The Job Seeker Manifesto:

"Tell Me About Yourself"

Secrets to Strategic Job Interviews

By Katherine Burik

Dan Toussant

The Interview Doctor®

Job Talk Press

Paperback ISBN: 978-0-9893787-9-6

ePDF ISBN: 978-0-9905934-0-9

ePUB ISBN: 978-0-9905934-1-6

Cover Design and Illustration by Justine Conklin
Book Design by Kim Krajci
Final Editing by Kim Krajci
Book Production by Bookmasters, Inc.

DEDICATION

I love when candidates call me excited that their preparation with this strategic approach to interviewing enabled them to speak with confidence for the first time. That is what The Interview Doctor® is all about!

I am so thankful to my wonderful daughter Marissa for her willingness to grow and change and especially to share her personal mantra of "Calm, Confident, and Courageous" with others who need a boost to look challenges full in the eye.

Life is an adventure! I know many people do not have the stomach for adventure, especially job search adventures. To them I offer this proven technique to tackle adventures with gusto, even when they are uncertain.

Adventure is worthwhile - Aristotle

— *Katherine Burik*

DEDICATION

For all the candidates we have coached through the Interview Doctor®, thanks for sharing your career planning and job-seeking challenges. Job seeking and especially interviewing is a valuable skill to learn. We appreciate the chance to understand this skill a little bit better every time we coach a candidate or a hiring manager.

- *Dan Toussant*

About This Series: How to Read This Book

Finding a new job can be hard. It can also be a rewarding and enlightening experience. The difference is how you approach the search.

After talking to many candidates at The Interview Doctor® and through our previous lives as human resource executives and recruiters in corporate America, we know candidates often share many of the same problems. We have some solutions that can help.

The key to a successful job search is to have a plan to distinguish yourself from other candidates. You have to be able to explain who you are and what you have to offer. Sadly, most candidates have absolutely no idea where to begin. While no one can figure that out for you, we can help guide you through the process.

The books in this series, *The Job Seeker Manifesto*, offers a step-by-step approach to finding a job including many strategies we learned from extensive experience throughout our careers. All the stories we share are true, reflecting real job seekers we worked with through The Interview Doctor®. We changed the names to protect our clients' privacy.

This is the third book in a series addressing job search starting with 1) creating a strategic plan, then 2) creating the tools necessary to display your talents including resumes and your LinkedIn profile, and 3) strategically designing how you describe yourself starting with the critical question, "Tell me about yourself".

Pick the topic or two that address your particular issue or read the entire series, depending on your specific needs and interests.

This third book provides you with a framework to use to prepare for job interviews. The words you choose should describe who you are, what you want and what you can contribute to the organization. We know this structure works but we realize that everyone's response to the important and difficult question, "Tell me about yourself" will be different.

Write in the margins. Take notes. Create worksheets. Challenge yourself to understand how to craft a Tell Me About Yourself Response to interview questions that will make you look great and feel confident.

Use these books to give yourself a head start over other candidates and find the job you love.

Table of Contents

DEDICATION ii

DEDICATION iii

How Is Comedy Like An Interview?......................................4

An Interview Is a Formula Too 6

Ten Tips for Beginners...8

Preparation is the Key 12

Anatomy of an Interview..16

About the Interview..19

Sad Stories 21

Autopsy of an Interview 22

Your Interview Style...24

Importance of Prior Preparation 25

Outcomes Can Change..31

Who Are You? 35

Interview Secrets...36

Filling Jobs - The Hiring Manager's Point of View 36

Begin With The End in Mind!..43

Define Who You Are..45

Begin by Knowing What You Want 47

Tell Me About Yourself...49

The Five Part Answer 50

The Elevator Speech 51

Part 1: A Few Facts 53

Activity 1 – A Few Facts 57

Have a Toolbox of Stories 58

Exercise 2 – Stories to Support My Facts 60

How to Use Stories 61

Part 2: What You Are Proud Of 64

Exercise 3 – Your Accomplishments for the Job 67

Part 3: Five Words 70

Exercise 4 – Finding Your 5 Words 73

Exercise 5 – Stories to Accompany Traits 75

Part 4: What You Want 77

Exercise 6 – What You Are Looking For 80

Part 5: Why They Should Hire You 82

Exercise 7 – Hire Me Because 83

Pull It All Together 84

When is it ok to take longer than a minute? 85

Random Interview Questions 90

Listening Is Critical 90

Preparation Lets You Observe and Anticipate 96

What are your strengths? 98

What is your weakness? 99

What do you want? 102

What are your career objectives? 103

What motivates you? 104

Describe your work style. 106

What was your top accomplishment? 107

What would others say about you? 107

Behavioral Questions...109

The Secret to Behavioral Questions 115

Questions about Planning and Organizing.................117

Questions about Sales Ability or Persuasiveness 121

Questions about Stress Tolerance 122

Deliberate Questions..123

Asking Your Own Questions 125

Pull it All Together..129

Preparation Makes You Confident 131

Discussion Questions...134

About The Interview Doctor, Inc. ® 137

Katherine Burik 138

Dan Toussant..140

Connect with us..141

References 142

The Job Seeker Manifesto Series Book 1

The
Job Search
Marketing Plan

Declare to the World How

You Will Find Your Next Job!

and

The Job Seeker Manifesto Series Book 2

Resume 3.0

Tools to Find Your Next Job

The Job Seeker's Manifesto:

"Tell me about yourself..."

We talk to people every day having problems finding a job. Sometimes they do not have the right tools. Sometimes their resumes are unattractive or disorganized. Sometimes they do not know what they want.

Most times, though, even folks with all the right tools equipped with a solid understanding of what they want have trouble. Their resume is good enough to get them an interview but they might have had six or seven interviews without snagging a job offer. Something is wrong.

Does this sound familiar? Did I just describe your job search?

We can almost guarantee you are doing something wrong during the interview. We can almost guarantee that we can fix it!

The key to a great interview is confidence that comes from knowing what to say. Learn the technique for answering the simple question, "Tell me a little about yourself." You will take control of the interview. You will develop confidence you never thought you had.

It takes practice and preparation to do well during interviews. Do not practice during a real interview. Invest time at the beginning to improve the way you handle interviews.

An interview is a terrible thing to waste!

Chapter 1

How Is Comedy Like An Interview?

The old joke starts, "A guy walks into a bar." This opening alerts the listener that something funny is supposed to happen next. This joke has many variations. You can change the joke around all sorts of ways to make it different from the last time.

Consider these oldies but goodies from A Man Walks into a Bar.com:

A fish walks into a bar. The bartender says, "What do you want?" The fish croaks, "Water".

A grasshopper walks into a bar. The barman looks at him and says, "Did you know there is a drink named after you?" "Really?" says the grasshopper. "There's a drink called Jeremy?"

A priest, a rabbi, and a vicar walk into a pub. The barman says, "Is this some kind of a joke?"

Funny, huh?

Every joke has a formula. There is the opening line, an observation about the character or the situation, then the punch line. Sometimes it is a long rambling story and sometimes it is a short, to the point joke. The combination of factors inside the joke makes it funny even though you know the joke is a formula. The formula gives structure and leads the listener from the opening to a point at the end, which is the laugh.

Comedians are expert storytellers. They appear so natural when you see them on TV or in concert. They stand up at the microphone and talk to the audience. They tell stories and jokes smoothly and with a purpose. You do not see all the preparation that went into making the joke come out funny at the end of the formula. You do not see all the hours spent practicing. The good ones are so confident. It seems like they are talking directly to you. You like them and want them to succeed.

Not every comedian is funny, just as not every storyteller can really tell a good story.

It is hard to put your finger on what might be missing, but something is missing. There are usually some visible signs. New comedians or bad ones are often not confident. They sweat a lot and stammer. The jokes have no structure and nothing is really funny. They do not really have anything to say. They just blather on. You feel bad for them but you know you do not want to see them again.

I cannot tell jokes well at all. Even stories are a little beyond me. I can hear it in my head but when I open my mouth, it comes out all wrong. Listeners sit there waiting for the punch line, disappointed when it comes out all wrong.

An Interview Is a Formula Too

What does joke telling have to do with interviewing? More than you think. Stay with me on this.

An interview is a formula with many different combinations. It invariably starts with, "Tell me about yourself." Where it goes from there often depends on you.

Candidates who interview well are confident and smooth. They have a story to tell and they tell it well. They use stories to draw a connection between what they have done and what they want. You like them and want them to be successful.

Candidates who interview poorly do not have much to say. They stammer and sweat, seldom making eye contact because they lack confidence. They talk but all you hear is blah, blah, blah. They do not clearly communicate what they want or why they should have it. You want them out of your office as fast as possible. You feel bad for them but you know you do not want to see them again.

Just like bad comedians, it is hard to put your finger on what is wrong but something is missing.

If you look closely, what is missing is structure. A poor interviewer, like a bad comedian, has not considered the structure behind the stories, he has not practiced enough beforehand, and usually does not really know what he wants out of the interview.

The formula behind a good joke or a good story is a structure that adds discipline. Just as structure and discipline ensures that the joke or story comes out the way the teller intends, discipline of preparation and structure is important to an interview. It is the great structure and preparation that makes you feel confident in everything you do. It is a circle. Structuring your presentation, whether a joke, story, or interview, requires discipline. Discipline means preparation. Preparation leads to confidence. Confidence brings the audience through the structure to the punch line!

Ten Tips for Beginners

Being a great comedian or interviewer takes a great deal of practice. These ten tips for beginning stand-up comedians from Ask.com can also help candidates preparing to interview for a job:

1. **Get on stage now**. Practice your interview responses as often as you can in front of real people. The more you practice, the more natural you will sound.

    Never pass up a chance to talk to someone about your background and what you want. Always be prepared to talk about yourself and your goals. You never know when the opportunity will strike but take advantage of every one.

    At a recent dinner party, I was seated next to someone I did not know. She asked questions about what I did. Because I was prepared to answer, a simple dinner party turned into a discussion about The Interview Doctor® and how we have fast action remedies for people searching for jobs. It was a chance for me to practice talking about what I do and who I am.

If I stammered and stuttered like a bad candidate or a bad comedian, she would have turned away. She only listened because I fluently told my story. My story had a beginning, middle, and an end. Get out and talk about yourself as often as you can.

Perhaps THE best way to practice your story is a Toastmasters club. We have seen the positive improvements in confidence, poise and coherence participants gain from this reasonably-priced public speaking program offers. For more information check out the Toastmasters International at www.toastmasters.org.

2. **Don't be afraid to bomb**. Your responses to an interview never come out of your mouth the way you intend unless you say it aloud

a lot. Practice is critical. The first few times
you say your responses out loud you will
sound silly even to yourself. You may
bomb, but you will get better over time.

3. **Keep up with your old stuff.** There is
   always room for improvement in your
   responses. Practice your tried-and-true
   responses along with responses to new
   questions you heard or are trying out.
   Analyze your past performances and
   identify areas for improvement.

4. **Don't steal or even borrow.** Comedians
   might stretch the truth a little to make a
   situation seem funnier, but we never, ever
   tell a lie or even exaggerate about our
   background. It is not worth it. It always
   ends in trouble, sometimes legal trouble. Be
   proud of your background. If you are not
   proud of what you have done, how can a
   company take you seriously?

5. **Watch your time.** Do not babble in
   interviews or in conversations with people
   you meet. Be respectful of time. Tell your
   story clearly and succinctly. Then be quiet.
   Be on time. End meetings on time.

6. **Tape yourself**. This is great advice for candidates. Make sure you like the way you sound and that the way you sound and look represents the person you want the employer to see. Make direct eye contact. Be aware of your image. Be purposeful in selecting the clothes you wear, your personal grooming, and mannerisms. Do not take chances. Taping yourself gives insight you will not get any other way.

7. **Hit the clubs**. Get out and meet people. Get your name out there. Networking at meetings and with people you meet leads to opportunities you will not find sitting in your basement office

8. **Make nice with the audience**. Be friendly and open so people you meet will like you. Be nice to everyone including the receptionist and the janitor. Companies hire people they like who they think will fit in with the other folks. Be the person they like.

9. **Carry a notebook.** You never know when you will need to write something down so be prepared, be aware, and take notes to review later. A notebook is a great place to record observations about your job search that strike you when you are out and about.

It also is a convenient prop if you get stuck waiting for someone. You can always look busy.

10. **Be yourself.** Let people see the real you. Be genuine. Relax. Let your preparation make you confident. Breathe.

Preparation is the Key

The common denominator between comedians and interviewing is preparation. Being prepared makes you confident so you can be yourself and be the person the hiring manager likes and wants to hire.

In our recruiting experience, we met many sad, poor candidates. These folks appeared to be qualified on paper or they would not have been invited in for an interview. But their presentation in person was poor. They did not know what to say. They could not describe their background. They did not have a story to tell. These folks were not hired.

I have changed jobs many times, more often than I like to talk about. I am a quiet person. I find it difficult to talk off the cuff. Meeting new people sometimes scares me to the core. I stammer and stutter while I am forming a good response. Interviews are the forum for quick talking, flashy folks, and not quiet folks like me.

The first few times I was laid off I was out of work for a long time. I did not know how to network. I was shy and quiet. I had trouble talking about myself. I stammered through interviews because I did not know what to say. My search process lacked discipline and my approach to interviews lacked structure. I needed to figure out a better way.

I did some deep soul searching about the interview process and about my performance. I realized that most interviews followed a pattern. Most hiring managers I spoke to asked the same questions.

That gave me an idea.

If I prepared my answers in advance and practiced, I might be more comfortable. Being more comfortable might help me express myself better during interviews.

I did not want to mess up any more interviews so I tried an experiment in a low risk situation at a few parties where I did not know many people.

Before the party, I read the Wall Street Journal and picked out about five or six topics I thought might come up in conversation. Then I walked up to someone I did not know and brought up one of the topics I prepared. To my surprise, the person responded! It sparked a conversation that I could handle because I did the research ahead of time. I felt more confident and the people I met seemed to respond positively to me.

I needed to try it next in interviews. I found all the possible questions that I thought I might be asked, and wrote answers to all of them. I said my answers aloud while looking in the mirror. I changed my self-talk from, "Who do you think you are?" to "Ok, I can do this." At the next interview, I repeated the answers I prepared and rehearsed in advance.

It worked! I was more relaxed. The words flowed out just as I practiced. I answered the questions well without stammering since I knew what I wanted to say. And the hiring managers liked me! I got a job!

I personally used this approach for the last 30 years in my own career. This approach works for many clients at The Interview Doctor®. It can work for you!

Chapter 2

Anatomy of an Interview

Good preparation begins with facing the truth. What do you sound like in an interview? We have interviewed thousands of people. We can tell the difference between a good interview and a bad interview. But can you?

If you have had more than a few interviews but never get the job offer, you are probably doing something wrong during the interview. Until you figure out what you are doing wrong, you will not be able to improve.

Listen to this interview and consider whether you would hire Nathan:

Interviewer: Good morning. I am glad you could come in today. Tell me a little about yourself.

Nathan: [*quiet, head down, no eye contact, very soft*]. Well, I work in accounting. [Long pause]

Interviewer: Uh huh. Tell me a little more.

Nathan: [*still quiet, not making eye contact, head down but starts talking*]. I am not sure what else you want to know. It has been a round-about path to get here. I grew up in a really small town in Ohio. I got my high school girl friend pregnant so we got married. We have two kids together but the marriage never really worked. So I left her. I really miss my kids. They live in Wisconsin now. I had to move to Cleveland to find work...

I really miss my kids. My youngest, Tom, is severely autistic so he needs special care, which is really expensive. His behavior is really awful. We can't take him anywhere...

I've held a bunch of bad jobs. I never seem to stay very long at any one thing. A friend told me about this program so I decided to get some extra training while I am out of work.

I really miss my kids. I wish I could see them more often but it takes a lot of hours to work in accounting, especially during the monthly close so I don't have a lot of time.

[*Pause*] I am not sure what else you want to know

Interviewer: Why do you want to leave your job?

Nathan: [*starts getting louder and obnoxious finally making a little eye contact*]. My last job was awful. The boss was a real jerk. Everyone hated him. I was there for about 4 months when he yelled at me in front of the group for putting this charge in the wrong account again. He was unreasonable too. He expected me to work at all hours and do all this stupid grunt work. The rules were stupid too.

The last straw was when he told me to come in to work on Labor Day to finish the close but I already told him I was planning to go to Wisconsin to see the kids for the weekend. I really gave it to him. I told him what he could do with his stupid job and then I walked out.

Interviewer: Hmmm... ok, what kind of position are you looking for now?

Nathan: I really need a position that pays well. I am behind in so many bills. I am about to get evicted if I don't get a good paying job right now, not to mention my son's medical bills. I would like to find a place where I can work for the rest of my life.

Interviewer: Why should we hire you?

Nathan: [*Pauses*]. I am not sure really. My friend told me to come here today. [*Pauses again*] What kinds of positions do you have open right now?

About the Interview

Would you hire Nathan?

What is going through the interviewer's mind at the end of this exchange? If you were the interviewer, would you offer Nathan a job? Probably not. I would not. No one will.

If Nathan continues to interview in this way, he will have a lot of trouble finding another job. If he gets lucky, he will find a menial, minimum wage job where his personal history and sad sack presentation are not important. He will probably complain to all his friends that it is age discrimination or that there are just no jobs out there.

This interaction is real. Nathan is a compilation of real men and women we have actually interviewed. He is a sad, pathetic character but he is not unusual. Folks like Nathan are not always unemployed either. We have interviewed many folks just like Nathan who are gainfully employed but trying to change jobs.

We share his story not to ridicule Nathan. He has had a difficult time and he really needs a job. I feel bad for him. In real interviews with people like Nathan, I often want to stop the interview and say, "Cut it out! Can't you see how sad you look? Don't you know no one will hire you with that attitude?" But I never do.

The truth is Nathan undermines his own future because he has absolutely no idea how to present himself during an interview. It is very sad too because he might be a good employee under the right circumstances.

We know there must be a gem of something useful in folks like Nathan but no one has the time to dig for it. We just pass Nathan on to the next interviewer and continue to search for the right candidate. We put Nathan out of our minds.

No interviewer will say what is really going through his or her mind about a candidate. They will never offer feedback or advice because they have no vested interest in the candidate. The interviewer is only interested in finding the one candidate who can solve this big problem – the person who can fill the job.

Sad Stories

Hiring managers have many stories about these sad characters. Sometimes we forget that these folks are not doing this on purpose.

I still remember a candidate I interviewed over 10 years ago. We will call him Tony to protect his identity. He was obnoxious. He wore a loud plaid blazer. He claimed credit for many accomplishments he could not substantiate. He claimed he could be the next VP of Marketing, even though he was interviewing for a Marketing Associate position.

Tony was simply awful. In retrospect, I think his loud exterior covered up a scared person inside. I thought he was simply awful and just wanted him out of my office. I gave no thought to Tony's feelings. Tony did nothing to endear himself to me or to demonstrate in any way that I should take him seriously. I even made fun of him later.

In hindsight, I feel bad for Tony. I do not know if Tony ever got the job he wanted. I suspect he never learned how to improve the way he interviewed. As far as I know, no one told Tony what he was doing wrong in the interview.

You do not want to be Tony or Nathan. Tony and Nathan might be talented people with a lot to offer. We just do not know from their interviews. And because the interviews were so spectacularly bad, we do not care to find out.

Autopsy of an Interview

Nathan is not necessarily doomed to permanent unemployment. He can fix his presentation and leave a better impression when he interviews. It is sometimes easier to see from the outside.

Let's list some things Nathan did wrong:

- **Body language.** Nathan's lack of eye contact and passive posture does not say confidence. He also does not listen, and is loud and obnoxious at times when he talks. That is no way to build a relationship that says Nathan will fit into that workplace. Nathan's body language signals problems.

- **About the job.** Nathan does not know anything about the job. He is only there because his friend told him to show up.

- **Too Much Information.** Clearly Nathan shared way too much personal information. No one wants to know about his kids or his personal troubles. It makes him look sad and pathetic. His family is his own business, important to Nathan but not important to anyone else, certainly not important to the interviewer.

- **Appropriate stories.** Nathan reveals kind of sketchy information about why he left his last job that makes him look unreliable and a little like a troublemaker. No one wants to hire trouble.

- **A turn off.** We never find out what Nathan can do or much about his background. Everything else is so off-putting we never get to the important stuff about how well he can do the job.

You probably know a man or woman like Nathan. Many people who are out of work long time, even high level executives, have been known to respond to interviews in this way. They get desperate. They will say or do anything to get a job, but desperation undermines their efforts.

Life is not easy and some people encounter roadblocks along the way. Your personal experiences are only your business. People listening to you talk will draw conclusions out of context. So keep personal information to yourself.

Your Interview Style

Are you Nathan? You might be Nathan if:

- Interviews often end after a short time. If you make a bad impression, the interviewer made up his or her mind in the first five minutes or less. They will conclude the interview after about 30 minutes or so, to avoid embarrassing you. Short interviews are usually a bad sign.

- You think you are supposed to talk to several people but you only talk to one person. That means the interviewer decided not to refer you to the next person and cut the interview short.

- If you think it went well but do not get a call back, you did not interview as well as you could.

- If you do not think you made a connection with the interviewer, you are probably right. Sometimes that is due to chemistry. Sometimes that is due to poor interviewing techniques.

- You get many first interviews but few second interviews. That means you must have a decent resume but something goes wrong in the interview.

- If you apply for promotions in your current company and get interviews but never get the promotion, you are probably doing something wrong in the interview.

Sound familiar? You are probably doing something wrong in the interview. This is not a permanent problem. You can learn how to interview better.

Importance of Prior Preparation

Good preparation can help anyone interview better. Preparation can make the difference between stagnation and promotion to candidates trying to get promoted from their current job.

Perhaps you are thinking, "These stories only apply to people who are out of work. I am working. I am sure I do a much better job interviewing than these sad sacks who are not working." You would be wrong.

Many people who are trying to change jobs while still working just do not know what to say. Many managers who hire people all the time forget that an interview has a structure with a formula. Successful sales people who know very well how to conduct a sales meeting forget that those meetings have a structure with a formula. The same concept of structure and formula works in all kinds of meeting, especially interviews. It just takes preparation.

Candidates often say the first thing that comes into their heads, revealing weaknesses or fears that undermine their efforts. This does not help their cause.

Let us consider some examples of talented people who want to change jobs but find they are having trouble during interviews.

Sheila's Story

Sheila is an engineer in her early 30s working for a large manufacturing company. She just finished her MBA and now wants to transition to a position in marketing but she is having trouble getting any traction. She is well thought of at her current job but for some reason keeps being passed over for promotions. She has an interview scheduled for next week for a Marketing Manager position in a great company. She does not want to waste this opportunity but she has no idea how to package her engineering background to show she can be successful in marketing.

The diagnosis? Sheila has not properly described her past experience in terms that can be understood by potential employers in her new field.

Sheila should highlight the ways she currently collaborates with marketing, projects she works on with marketing and research and development cross functional teams, financial impact of ideas she put into play that improve margins or sales. Sheila needs stories about the impact that her work as an engineer has had on marketing and sales results. She must translate her engineering activities into marketing terms using statistics and results that marketing people will understand and value.

Tom's Story

Tom has managed a wholesale distribution branch for the last 20 years. He interviewed for a Branch Manager position in another city for a larger branch. He was well thought of and had great results at his current branch. He showed up to the interview with a resume printed on red paper, dressed in a flannel shirt. He leaned back in the chair and stretched out. He acted like he was making himself comfortable but nothing about Tom seemed like he was confident.

The interview went something like this:

Interviewer: So, tell me a little about yourself.

Tom: [*quiet, looking out the window, no eye contact, smiling*] You have my resume. What more do you want to know?

Interviewer: Why don't you tell me a little about your background?

Tom: Ok, well as my resume indicates, I grew up in Pennsylvania. I went to college for a while but had to drop out for financial reasons. Then I got drafted so I joined the Air Force. After I returned, I worked a bunch of odd jobs in construction until I got offered a position for the construction materials distributor. I worked in various warehouse positions then in sales until I had the chance to step in for the manager.

Interviewer: What are you looking for now?

Tom: I thought that was obvious. I am here to interview for the open position in West Virginia. I want to be closer to my family in southwest Pennsylvania. My folks are getting older and need me to be closer.

Interviewer: Why should we hire you?

Tom: I am available and willing to move to West Virginia. What else is there?

Tom did not get the job. He was not sure why.

The diagnosis? It is not that Tom did not take the interview seriously, although he gave that impression. He was not being glib or arrogant, although he gave that impression. Tom simply did not know what to do. He was out of his comfort zone. He does not like to talk about himself. It seems too much like bragging. He thinks his results should stand for themselves, which is why he did not offer details. He assumed that since he was interviewing inside his own company that the interviewers would know about his results so he did not offer details.

Tom is actually a great storyteller. He has great rapport with his customers and employees. He just has trouble translating his normal friendly self into an interview persona. He needs to find the stories about his experiences that highlight his success. Telling stories will help Tom feel more comfortable and less like he is bragging.

Tom needs to understand how interviews work from the candidate side. It is ironic that Tom has interviewed people as a branch manager but he has not been on the candidate side for years. He can get much more comfortable by preparing his answers in advance and practicing them until they roll off his tongue just like the stories he tells with such gusto.

Outcomes Can Change

How can we restructure Nathan's interview response to make his interview more successful? Let us listen in to Nathan after he was coached by The Interview Doctor®. This is the same candidate with the same facts. We will call him Nathan 2.0.

The interviewer asks the same questions. Some of the information Nathan 2.0 shares did not come up in the first interview because Nathan did not realize this information was important or that he could structure his response in this way. For this reason, the same person (Nathan) can sound like a different person.

What do you think?

Interviewer: Good morning. I am glad you could come in today. Tell me a little about yourself.

Nathan 2.0: [*sits up straight with good eye contact, smiling*]. Good morning! It is great to be here! I am from Canton, Ohio where I went to Walsh University for a degree in Accounting. I relocated to Wisconsin with my family then moved back to northeast Ohio for a better position a few years ago. I am completing my

CPA credentials at University of Akron right now.

I am hard working, determined, analytical, friendly, and team oriented.

I am particularly proud of changes I made to the general ledger reports at my last company which allowed us to shorten the close by one day.

I am looking for a position where I can use my accounting skills to help a company stay organized.

I know I will be a solid contributor to your accounting team.

Interviewer: Why did you leave your last job?

Nathan 2.0: I left my last position when the company restructured the accounting department. Leaving also allowed me to devote my full attention to completing my CPA credentials while I find a new position.

Interviewer: What kind of position are you looking for?

Nathan 2.0: I am looking for an accounting position that uses my background and experience to stay organized. I know I can make a contribution.

Interviewer: Why should we hire you?

Nathan 2.0: I am hard working, determined, and well organized. I bring great experience and background and I know I could do a great job.

What do you think of Nathan 2.0? How did his responses this time differ from the first interview? What did he do well? What did you learn about this candidate?

- Nathan 2.0 is much more composed. He makes good eye contact this time.
- He speaks clearly and knows what he wants to say. He does not wander all around. He gets directly to the point. He knows what he wants to say.
- He does not share personal information. It is still true that his family is a mess, he had kids too early, and he quit his last job. This personal information is only Nathan's business. He is not required to share that

information with anyone during an interview.

- He focuses on his business experience and education rather than his personal experience. He points to accomplishments related to the position he wants and makes a case for why he should be hired.
- Nathan 2.0 does not share the sordid details of how or why he left his last job. It does not make Nathan 2.0 look good so he adjusts his story. It is true that after Nathan was fired they restructured the accounting department so they would not have to refill the position. That happens a lot. This kind of reshuffling can legitimately be called a "restructuring". Interviewers will accept this explanation and move on. Nathan 2.0 shares information he wants the interviewer to know. He does not lie or exaggerate. Some of the information Nathan 2.0 shares did not come up in the first interview because Nathan did not realize this information was important or that he could structure his response in this way.

Would you hire Nathan 2.0? Nathan 2.0 is much more likely to get a job offer with the revised response to typical interview questions. Getting beyond the first interview increases the chances that the hiring decision will be made on the chemistry between Nathan 2.0 and the hiring manager, which is exactly what Nathan 2.0 wants.

Who Are You?

Be critical for a moment. Look at your recent interviews. Do you see yourself in Nathan? It is not the end of the world as long as you are willing to change the way you handle interviews.

Poor interviewers like Nathan are not confined to the ranks of lower level unemployed people. We find people like Nathan everywhere. Some Nathan clones are executives, even company presidents so caught up in their own stories that they are unaware of the impression they leave. You may find a Nathan as a middle managers. They can be found in any field at every level.

You can choose to be Nathan 2.0 with some simple technique and structure. You do not want to sound like Nathan. Enough said.

Chapter 3

Interview Secrets

Here is the deep dark secret of interviewing. Most hiring managers are bad at recruiting and interviewing. They are very busy and often poorly trained. They would give anything to have a candidate with something to say. It would make the hiring manager so happy.

Filling Jobs - The Hiring Manager's Point of View

Most people think that an interview is a power situation. The hiring manager has the power to hire. The candidate wants the job so that means the candidate must have little power.

Is this really true? What if there is a way to equalize the situation so the candidate is not always the underdog? Would you be interested?

Let us consider an open position from the hiring managers' point of view.

There are likely two main reasons a position is open:

1. Someone on the team left the job through termination, promotion, or resignation.
2. Work is so plentiful that a new person has been approved to be added to the team.

In both situations, there is more work to be done than people to do the work. Someone, likely the hiring manager, must absorb the extra work. This creates a problem for the hiring manager.

Hiring takes a lot of time. You have to find candidates, shuffle through resumes and phone screen, pick a few people to interview, and find people to help you interview, schedule the interview, and then hope you pick the right candidate.

Harriet's Story

Harriet is an Engineering Manager with EFG Company, a large international company that offers complete design, engineering and manufacturing services to technical customers. She has a team of eight engineers who design wire harnesses. She is constantly busy making sure as many as a dozen projects move towards completion. Lately the pressure has been worse. Her best engineer, Dave, resigned last month and she is up to her eyeballs making sure the team does not miss any deadlines even though they are working short-handed.

Stacey, her HR Manager, has offered numerous times to help her find another candidate. She even outlined a job description and ad to get the recruiting started but Harriet just cannot seem to find the time.

Stacey went ahead and placed an ad on CareerBuilder. She found some interesting candidates, even conducted some phone screens. Harriet saw the resumes but has not had time to set up interviews.

Meanwhile Harriet gets further and further behind. She works longer hours to fill in for Dave plus she has delegated some of Dave's work to the other engineers but clearly she needs a replacement now. Stacey is trying to keep those candidates warm but one by one, the candidates are finding other opportunities.

The diagnosis? Harriet is working on short term priorities at the expense of long term results. She is trying to keep up with the short term work when she should be focusing on the job search. She needs to participate in her own rescue and prioritize the recruiting process. The only way Harriet gets any resolution to this problem is to find a replacement for Dave. Unfortunately the candidates do not see how overworked Harriet is. The candidates get the impression that the company (through Harriet) does not value them.

Then there is paperwork. You have to make sure you have the right forms filled out, check references, and put together an offer. You have to get the proper approval at the beginning, middle, and end of the process.

Jaxson's Story

Jaxson is Recruiting Manager at a large regional accounting firm. He is trying to fill a staff accountant position that came open at his office but he is having a hard time getting the attention of the hiring manager. He took the initiative to create a requisition and get the job posted internally as the policy requires. He had a talk with the hiring manager and it seemed like everything was approved. He posted the job and started receiving resumes from interesting candidates. After phone screening, he presented five candidates to the hiring manager for his review.

After waiting for six weeks to get feedback from the hiring manager, Jaxson set up interviews for the three candidates the hiring manager wanted to see. After the interviews, the hiring manager changed his mind about the position requirements! Now the hiring manager wants to see candidates with tax experience instead of audit experience. None of the previous candidates had audit experience because that kind of experience was not previously required.

Jaxson has to tell the previous candidates that the position specifications have changed putting them out of contention. Then he has to repost the job with the new specifications. Hopefully this time the hiring manager knows what he wants!

Even when the right candidate is found for the right position that needs to be filled, sometimes it takes time to order the right tools and make sure the work area is set up to accommodate the new hire.

This is a lot of hassle. All the while the work piles up, everyone in the department, including the hiring manager, is overloaded trying to achieve the department goals while shorthanded.

It is awful. No one is happy.

Even if everything goes smoothly according to plan, the hiring manager often wonders if the candidate represents the correct choice. Will this person fit into the team? Will the person perform as advertised? Are we making a mistake by hiring this person?

Sophia's Story

Sophia is the regional sales director at a major manufacturing company. She has an opening on her sales team covering a large metropolitan area. She interviewed about ten people over the last five months and thinks she finally found the right candidate in Chad. Chad has a good sales background. The references checked out just fine. Something is nagging at the back of Sophia's mind. She is a little concerned about whether Chad will get along with customer service. This is a big deal since sales and customer service work so closely together. She asked the lead customer service representative on the team to interview Chad. The response was good but something is still bothering Sophia. This makes Sophia drag her feet more than a

*little. Once a long time ago, Sophia made a bad
hiring choice that ended up costing time and money
when she fired that person. She does not want to
make the same mistake. She doubts herself. She just
does not know what to do.*

All in all, the hiring process puts a big burden
on hiring managers. The last thing on the hiring
manager's mind is preparing for an interview.
They open their drawer and pull out a standard
list of question they found online years ago. They
print off your resume just before you walk in.
Then they paste on a big grin and pretend to be
important and powerful.

But they are not.

They might act powerful on the outside but
inside they are a bundle of nerves like Harriet,
Jaxson and Sophia. They have too much work to
do and not enough time or resources to get it
done. They are full of fear.

Hiring managers would love to talk about
something more substantial than the standard list
of questions and the silly responses they typically
get from most candidates. They would rather talk
about what you want to talk about. It is less work
for them.

Coincidently, you are most comfortable talking about topics you know a lot about, like yourself. You will do the hiring manager a big favor by giving him or her the chance to ask interesting follow up questions to fascinating nuggets of information you place in front of him instead of the routine questions they would have asked.

The trick to a great interview is being prepared to tell stories about your experiences so the hiring manager can relax and get to know you better as a person. This gives you power to control the interview. It also takes the burden off the hiring manager to pretend to be omnipotent.

Begin With The End in Mind!

Your job search starts with what you want. If you do not know exactly what you want, you will flounder. No one will define it for you. You will never be able to interview properly if you do not know what you want. Every word that comes out of your mouth strategically aligns your experiences with the available position. You cannot do that unless you know what you want.

Padma's Story

Padma has all the right credentials. She is in her mid-20s with an MBA and a BS in Industrial Engineering from Purdue. She is smart and pleasant but she just could not find a job. She landed interviews because her credentials were good but something always went wrong during the interview. She seldom got a second interview and never got an offer.

Padma came to The Interview Doctor® for help. We asked her the question: "Tell me about yourself."

Padma's response: "I will do anything. I work hard, and I have been successful in the past. I know I can do whatever you need me to do."

Ouch. Padma's response is vague. Not only that, it is not really true. I am sure that are many things that Padma does not want to do but Padma is afraid to limit her opportunities by saying what she wants.

The irony is that it is easier to get a job by limiting the job possibilities to only those kinds of jobs you really want to do.

Hiring managers are busy. They hope that you are the candidate to fill the job so they can get back to their regular job and you can take some work off their desks. They can only evaluate you based on what you say you want. They do not have time to look closely at your background and try to figure out how they can utilize your unique variety of experiences. You need to package it for the hiring manager up front so they know immediately what you have to offer.

The diagnosis: Padma is not being specific enough. She must draw a line between her experience and the vacant job. If she does not make that connection then who will?

Define Who You Are

Sarah's Story

Sarah is a college professor in her 40s trying to find a new position. She has a big interview coming up in a few weeks. This is the job she really wants. She is qualified. She wants to have a great interview,so she came to The Interview Doctor to prepare.

We asked Sarah, "Tell me about yourself." She stammered and stuttered. Finally, in a squeaky little girl voice she choked out, "Well, I am kind of shy and …. I am not sure what to say."

Imagine the response if she said that in an interview? She might have too. Other candidates have said had that response. Sad but true.

The diagnosis: Sarah did not express herself well. She must be able to define what she can offer and what she wants with confidence and clarity. She believes she is qualified for the job. Now her task is to make the hiring manager believe it too. In addition to finding the right words to describe her qualifications, she must find the grown up confident voice with which to say the words.

Structure your responses to any interview question from the perspective of what you want. We call this your purpose or mission. You must describe what you want and who you are in just a few words in a minute or less.

Justin's Story

Justin is a successful graphics designer in his 30s looking for a new position. He had all the tools in place: a great track record, a good LinkedIn profile 100% complete, a website displaying his work, and a great resume. But he lacked confidence in his ability to talk about himself. He has no idea how to answer the threshold question, "Tell me about yourself." He is a quiet person and finds it difficult to make conversation or talk off the cuff.

Having all the tools in place without the ability to talk about them or answer basic questions undermines his search.

The diagnosis: Justin lacks confidence and clarity. He must be able to describe what he wants succinctly. He must prepare and internalize responses to the most frequently asked questions so he can minimize improvisation to maximize confidence.

Begin by Knowing What You Want

You must be able to describe succinctly in a few sentences exactly what you are looking for. Then you can use this information to build a comfortable way of responding to common questions. Every response to common questions will have a strategic purpose to establish the links between what you want, what you have to offer, and the position in front of you.

Knowing what you want also gives you a benchmark to compare against available job offers. If you do not know what you want then how do you know if that job offer is the right job for you?

Knowing what you want provides the platform upon which to build almost all responses to potential interview questions that come your way.

Answers roll off your tongue because you thought about them in advance. You can edit your responses and practice them aloud. We like to say that you should practice your responses out loud until your dog stops laughing at you! You practice at home in front of a friend or a mirror so you do not practice in front of a real hiring manager.

When you are prepared, then you can focus on what else is going on around you. You can structure answers to fit the question because you anticipate the questions they will ask. You do not have to figure everything out off the top of your head during the interview, just fine tune.

When you are prepared, you can control the interview.

Chapter 4

Tell Me About Yourself

We start with "Tell me about yourself" because it is the threshold question which is almost always asked first in the interview or in most conversations when you network. Designing an effective response to this question gives you a solid start to any conversation.

Your response to this question provides a formula to use with other responses and stories you wish to tell about yourself during the interview. Responses to all questions should have a beginning, middle, and end that demonstrate your experience and expertise.

Since you do not know yet which parts of your background are most important to the interviewer, your response to "Tell me about yourself," includes tidbits that the hiring manager will find irresistible. The rest of the interview will be filled with follow up questions on topics you love to discuss.

Be a person hiring managers want to talk to and want to work with. People hire people they want to be around. You must be confident and be able to express what you have to offer. If you do not believe it then why should a hiring manager believe it?

The Five Part Answer

Create a great answer by breaking your Tell Me About Yourself Response down into its basic elements then building a compact response that covers a lot of territory in a short time. We use a formula, just like a comedian building a joke.

We break the answer to "Tell me about yourself" into five parts. This allows you to consider each section, edit carefully, then identify stories you want to tell as follow ups. The stories are critical.

Your response should take no more than a minute or so, definitely not more than two minutes. That means you only have a little bit of time on each element. This is an overview, not a speech. You can never be sure exactly what portion of your response will spark interest from the hiring manager so just include teasers. Save the details for follow up.

The five parts to a great Tell Me About Yourself Response are:

1. A few facts
2. An accomplishment
3. Five words to describe yourself
4. What you are looking for
5. Why you should have the job

We will walk through each part in subsequent sections. At the end, you will assemble all five parts into a cohesive, one-minute response to the question.

The Elevator Speech

If you think this sounds like an "elevator speech," you are right! The concept of an elevator speech has been around a long time. What would you say if the President of the United States stepped into the elevator with you? What if he said, "Tell me a little about yourself?" What would you say?

You cannot be silent. You cannot babble. You have to stand up straight, make eye contact, have a strong handshake, and have something to say. You have only a few seconds. What is the most important thing you want the other person to know?

Maybe you are proud of your kids. Do you tell the Very Important Person that you are proud of your kids?

Maybe? Is that the most important thing you want this Very Important Person to know? Or do you say you were born in a log cabin in northern Minnesota? Probably not. You tell the Very Important Person something you want them to remember about you, something about you that means something to the Very Important Person.

Your response to "tell me about yourself" should contain key information you want the Very Important Person to remember about you that is important to the Very Important Person.

The solution is to craft an answer to this question scientifically. Put these five parts together into a seamless 30 second to one-minute statement. This becomes your pitch, your elevator speech. Let's get started.

Chapter 5

Part 1: A Few Facts

You want to set the stage so the interviewer has a basic understanding of where you come from. If you wanted to, you could include where you were raised, what college you went to for undergrad and graduate school, and something about your profession and perhaps your leadership experience.

This part is only one fifth or less of one minute so you must consider carefully which facts you want to include. Include facts that relate to your job goal.

Katherine's Elevator Speech

I am from Chicago - born and raised, third generation. I got my BA from Northwestern University and my MS in Industrial Relations from Loyola University of Chicago. I have worked in Human Resources and Labor Relations my entire career. For the last 23 years, I have been a Director or VP reporting to the President of various companies ranging from manufacturing, to service, to distribution.

Keep it short and to the point. Do not describe every element on your resume, just some basic facts. It is not necessary to walk the interviewer through your resume. If they want more information about something in particular, they will ask.

This is a teaser, not a novel. At the start of an interview, you cannot be sure what will be interesting to the listener so you give them a short overview and wait to hear what interests them.

You might want to include some things that you think will intrigue the interviewer.

Katherine likes to say she is from Chicago because many times people from Ohio (where she lives now) ask her about it. She likes to talk about Chicago and knows they will ask, so it becomes a topic of conversation during the interview – something Katherine can speak with confidence about as opposed to something the interviewer comes up with that Katherine is less familiar with. Neat trick, huh? These kind of conversation starters create a dialog right away. Rapid and regular two-way conversing are a secret to good interviewing. These 'basic fact' type ideas help build quick camaraderie.

Dan likes to bring up the Akron Rubber Ducks because it is a funny name for a baseball team; most people, men or women, find it amusing, and that starts the conversation with a smile.

One client, David, once complained that when he gave his elevator speech the interviewers always stopped him to talk about the fact that he was from Jamaica. He sounded annoyed and wanted to know how to get interviewers to listen to his entire pitch.

My response, "Are you crazy?" Why would you want to avoid talking about something that everyone thinks is fascinating? He has stories about growing up in Jamaica. He can talk for hours about it. This simple fact could be the topic he uses to build rapport with hiring managers. When they ask questions about Jamaica, they are not asking questions off the list of most frequently asked questions. The interviewer is trying to learn more about David. This topic could lead to a lengthy conversation that turns David into a real person instead of one of many resumes.

Now you try it! Complete the following exercise to help get you started.

Activity 1 – A Few Facts

List five or six facts about your background that you want people to know about you or that will prompt questions from the interviewer:

1._____

_____

_____

2._____

_____

_____

3._____

_____

_____

4._____

_____

_____

5._____

_____

_____

6._____

_____

_____

Have a Toolbox of Stories

Every fact must have a story behind it. You should be prepared to talk in greater detail about those facts if asked. Only if asked-do not elaborate yet.

Behind the scenes while you are preparing, you should also organize stories that you would like to share, when you are asked. Put those stories in your virtual toolbox so you can take them out when you need them during the interview.

Every candidate needs a toolbox. Your interview toolbox is like a golf bag if you are a golfer, a tackle box if you are a fisherman, or a computer bag if you work with computers. The bag contains tools that you might need under certain circumstances. You might not need them at all but if you do, you want to have those tools available.

Imagine being a golfer without a putter? Impossible. There is certainly a putter in that bag, along with extra irons, extra woods, some extra tees and balls just in case you hit one into the water.

In my computer bag, I have extra power cords for my computer, Kindle, telephone, and other assorted electronics. I have USB cords, headphones, a cloth to wipe the screen, and extra memory sticks. I would not dream of leaving home without these tools.

Every candidate needs a bag of stories and examples to illustrate your experience and expertise.

Now add a story for each fact you think is important. You do not need to tell the whole story right now. You will use the stories to support the experiences and expertise you describe about yourself.

Exercise 2 – Stories to Support My Facts

Use the following space to identify and briefly outline the stories or examples that demonstrate the qualities you identified in the previous activity.

Story 1:

_____

_____

_____

Story 2:

_____

_____

_____

Story 3:

_____

_____

_____

Story 4:

_____

_____

_____

Story 5:

_____

_____

_____

Story 6:

_____

_____

_____

How to Use Stories

These stories should not be long. Practice telling the whole story in 2 minutes or less. Every story should have a beginning, middle, and an end. There should be a point to the story at the end that makes you look good and supports the claims you make. This is what you learned.

For example, I use a fact that I have reported to presidents on senior staffs for over 20 years. Someone might ask, "Really? Tell me about your first experience." I am prepared with a story. I often tell this story. I wrote it down long ago and still use it just like this:

Katherine's Story

I became Director of Human Resources at the age of 30 years old working for a wonderful old German fellow named Dieter. At our first staff meeting, Dieter closed and locked the door (as was his habit) sat down and put his head in his hands and said, "Now what the heck are we going to do."

Evidently I did not ask the right questions when I was interviewing. I did not realize the company was in serious financial trouble. I spent the next three years restructuring the business and making changes that resulted in putting one-third of the company out of business, selling off one-third to a competitor, and selling one-third to a management buy-out group. It was quite an experience for my first leadership role.

This story is usually well received. Listeners often find it humorous because I tell the story at my own expense to demonstrate that I work well under pressure, learn from my mistakes, and solve problems. It also shows I was involved in some critical business changes early in my career. I chose the story for strategic reasons and structured it to show certain characteristics that position me in a certain way in the listeners' eyes.

The stories you select should be chosen just as carefully. Pick your words carefully. Write down your answer in advance and edit it until you can say it in a minimum of words so it sounds natural. Stories should take only a minute or two to tell. Do not ramble all over. Be strategic so you always have a point and the story makes you look good and leads to further conversation.

Chapter 6

Part 2: What You Are Proud Of

Since you are designing your own response to this question, take the opportunity to describe an accomplishment related to the job for which you are interviewing. This provides a direct topic for discussion that gets you immediately into your qualifications for the job, but you are not doing it directly. You are smoothly going from some facts about your background into something related to your background that you are proud of.

You want to select something from your toolkit of experiences that relates to the job for which you are interviewing. We select an accomplishment about something we really want to talk about that should be irresistible to the interviewer. You want them to ask you follow up questions about this accomplishment.

We want them to say, "Gosh, how did you do that?" We want them to think, "I want someone on my team who can do that."

Nathan 2.0, the accountant who interviewed so badly at first, includes an accomplishment in his response. He said he was proud he suggested changes to the general ledger process that resulted in reducing time to close each month by one day. Nathan 2.0 uses an example from his past that is true, because we always tell the truth. It is intriguing to the hiring manager because it is related to the job he wants to obtain. It is something he likes to talk about that is not easy to do.

Sarah, the college professor, can say she is particularly proud of the online master's degree program she created for her last university. Since this is Sarah's favorite topic, she is very comfortable telling stories about her online degree program. It was a difficult task to achieve. She knows people she interviews with will want to know more. It is irresistible.

Justin, the graphics designer, can say he is particularly proud of the marketing campaign he created that won an award and increased sales by 25%. Justin will select an accomplishment connected to the job he wants to obtain that makes him look great. He has many accomplishments from which to choose. He can talk confidently and freely about these accomplishments which makes interviewing easier for a shy person like Justin.

Now you try it!

Exercise 3 – Your Accomplishments for the Job

List one or two accomplishments related to the position you want to obtain. Use the posting describing the job to help identify what is important. Then, because every accomplishment has a story behind it, you need to identify a story for each accomplishment.

Accomplishment 1:

_____

_____

_____

_____

Story for Accomplishment 1:

_____

_____

_____

_____

_____

Remember the story needs four parts: a beginning, middle, and an end that relates to what you want and makes you look good, plus what you learned. It should be only a few minutes long so you need to write down your story and edit it until it fits the time limit. Then practice it aloud until the story just flows off your tongue.

Continue identifying stories until you have one to accompany each of the accomplishments you want to stress.

Accomplishment 2:

_____

_____

_____

_____

_____

Story for Accomplishment 2:

_____

_____

_____

_____

_____

_____

Accomplishment 3:

_____

_____

_____

_____

_____

Story for Accomplishment 3:

_____

_____

_____

_____

_____

Accomplishment 4:

_____

_____

_____

_____

Story for Accomplishment 4:

_____

_____

_____

_____

_____

Accomplishment 5:

_____

_____

_____

_____

_____

Story for Accomplishment 5:

_____

_____

_____

_____

_____

_____

Chapter 7

Part 3: Five Words

A common, frequently asked question is, "Tell me five words that describe you." We like to put that information out there right up front, before interviewers have a chance to ask. We do this for several reasons.

The process of identifying five words requires thinking carefully about who you are and what you have to offer. Without careful thorough thought in advance, a candidate can come up with three words off the top of their heads. A little struggle brings a fourth. But the task becomes very difficult to think of five words that really mean something to you off the top of your head. By thinking of these words in advance, you look prepared. Being prepared increases your confidence and makes you look better.

Another reason to include the five words is more subtle. We believe it is very important that you are happy and feel comfortable at your next job. By including a few words to describe yourself, you are laying out who you are. If you are not the right person for the job, you certainly do not want to put yourself in a place where you are uncomfortable, no matter how much you need or want a new job.

Everyone's five words are different because everyone is an individual. Katherine says she is smart, high energy, a team player, a problem solver, and she likes to have fun. She is not everyone's cup of tea. There are workplaces that do not value Katherine's energy. She would be unhappy in a workplace where she had to follow the rules without having any input to solving problems. Being out of sync leads to conflict and frustration, which often gets someone fired. Katherine has been there and has the t-shirt.

There are workplaces and management teams that do not value people with Katherine's behavior style. She does not want to work in a place that will not value what she brings. Neither do you.

Let's look at a few more examples.

Kermit's words are: amiable, talkative, energetic, friendly, and outgoing. These are totally different words than Katherine.

Dan's words are: networker, high-energy, creative, amiable and strategic. Most of these words are different from Katherine and Kermit.

These differences are not good and they are not bad. They just are. The word choice reflects that people will behave in different ways from each other.

If you have ever worked in a place you hated where you felt unvalued and unappreciated then you probably worked in a place that was out of sync with your preferred behavior style. Your five words did not fit with your colleagues or the work culture. It happens. If it has happened to you then you probably understand the power of the five words.

This is important stuff. It is important that you find a workplace that values who you are. You want to know right away if you are not the right person for that particular workplace. There is a place for everyone. It is your job to find the place that is right for you.

Now you try it!

Exercise 4 – Finding Your 5 Words

What five words would you use to describe
yourself? List the five words that best describe you
in the spaces below.

1. _____

2. _____

3. _____

4. _____

5. _____

Exercise 5 – Stories to Accompany Traits

Since you do not know what portion of your response will be interesting to the interviewer, you must be prepared to describe what you mean by the words you say.

For example, an interviewer might ask Katherine, "What do you mean by 'high energy?'" Katherine needs to be prepared with a story to describe what she means.

What kind of story could you tell about each of your five words?

Story for Trait 1

_____

_____

_____

_____

_____

_____

Story for Trait 2

_____

_____

_____

_____

_____

Story for Trait 3

_____

_____

_____

_____

_____

_____

Story for Trait 4

_____

_____

_____

_____

_____

Remember you do not use the story unless someone asks. But you need to be prepared.

Chapter 8

Part 4: What You Want

Part of who you are is what you want. Start off the interview right by saying what you want. It is important that the person you are talking to knows what you want so they can start thinking about you in that role right away.

Your answer to this part should relate to the job you are interviewing for. Nathan 2.0 wants a job in accounting. Sarah wants a job teaching college level education courses in an online program. John wants a job in logistics. Justin wants a job in graphics design. Say exactly what you want. Otherwise, you will never get what you want.

A word of warning: Be sure what you say is the same job as the job you are interviewing for. If you do not, the interviewer will be confused about why you are there. For example, if John was interviewing for a position as an industrial engineer and he said he wanted to be a musician, it would make him look silly. If Justin was interviewing an applicant for a position in marketing who said she wanted a position in graphics design, Justin would look confused.

Your response here is strategic.

Consider it this way. Let's say Katherine was interviewing for a position as VP Human Resources in a company that wanted someone to specialize in talent development. She has extensive human resource experience with lots of accomplishments in her portfolio. She could say many things but in this case she should say:

> *I am looking for a position as a Human Resource executive focused on talent development.*

She wants the interviewer to say to himself, "Gosh, this person is looking for a position just like the one we have!" They are not likely to think she is making it up or being manipulative. Katherine's experience, perhaps like yours, can be adjusted to emphasize one aspect or another depending on what she needs to emphasize.

If she were interviewing for a position with the same title in a company that had personnel problems, she would give a different response:

I am looking for a position as a Human Resource executive in an organization focused on resolving problems through people.

Perhaps it is a subtle difference but it is important. Align your answer with the position in front of you. Say what you want very succinctly. Do not go into detail. Be simple and clear. Right to the point.

Don't talk about how you want a long career with such a great company. No one cares. Just continue to relate your experience to the available job.

Now you try it!

Exercise 6 – What You Are Looking For

What you are looking for is both the job you want
to do and the position the company is offering. In
the space provided, create a statement that
combines a position description with your
qualifications and interests.

I am looking for a position as:

_____

_____

Where I can:

_____

_____

_____

_____

_____

Now, prepare a story about why you want this
job, perhaps how this job fits with your
background:

_____

_____

_____

_____

_____

You will only use this story if you are asked. But have it ready just in case.

Chapter 9

Part 5: Why They Should Hire You

This is the easiest part. It is important to state right up front why they should hire you.

They should hire you because you bring demonstrated experience that will make the company grow, or make the company successful, or solve a particular problem. Relate your experience to the job.

Keep it short and simple. Just a few words about what you can do for them.

For example, Katherine usually says,

"I have the demonstrated experience to solve people problems so the organization thrives."

Short and sweet. Right to the point. This kind of a response fits most situations but may be adjusted as needed.

The follow up questions usually asks for more details on your experience. That is fine. You have a story prepared how your experience with XYZ Company doing SOMETHING SPECIAL that worked out great and could transfer to this company.

Now you try it!

Exercise 7 – Hire Me Because

This is where you identify the most impressive thing about you. You are the person they want because...

_____

_____

_____

_____

_____

_____

_____

Chapter 10

Pull It All Together

You have written out all your responses to each of the five parts. Now you need to run it all together and say it aloud from the beginning. Time yourself. Remember this should take about one minute:

- My name is ...

- And I'm [your few facts...]

- I am particularly proud of .... [accomplishment related to this position]

- I am [string together your five words]

- I am looking for a position as [insert what you want] doing [something related to your background that relates to this position]

- I have the demonstrate expertise to make this organization successful [or something that makes sense for you about why you should get this job]

How does that feel? Most Interview Doctor® clients say that having a structure like this feels much better than winging it.

The first few times you say it, your response will sound awkward and take probably take more than a minute. So edit your response and practice out loud until it sounds smooth and natural and takes about a minute.

When is it ok to take longer than a minute?

It is almost always possible to structure your response to this question in about a minute. Even the most senior executive can do it. It is a good exercise in discipline. To make this happen you must understand what you have to offer and how you want other people to see you. Everyone should be able to do it.

There are always exceptions. Occasionally we work with clients with very complex backgrounds or folks who are very detail oriented.

Paul's Story

Paul was a vice president with a complex operations background. He is also very detail oriented. He has quite a lot to offer and many accomplishments. His first few attempts at "Tell me about yourself" took almost five minutes. It was very difficult to cut down his response but eventually he got his answer down to one minute thirty seconds. This worked well for him even though it was a little longer than most.

Paul used his response while networking, in interviews, and at meetings. Taking the time to reduce his experience to a manageable 90 seconds helped people understand him faster. Then they could get straight to the more detailed discussions about aspects of Paul's background. It was not necessary to lay out every experience to demonstrate his skill. He only needed an overview, or an outline, that could lead to further discussions. This strategy worked well for Paul. He ended up with a great promotion in his next position.

Some job seekers just talk too much or speak to quickly.

Diane's Story

Diane talked a mile a minute. She had a lot to talk about. Her background was great. After she failed to get two promotions she really wanted, that everyone said she was well qualified for, she realized she might be the problem. She must find a different approach to interviewing.

Diane needed to speak much more slowly. She was an extrovert and thoughts just came rushing out of her. Slowing down was very difficult for her. I thought the structure of "Tell me about yourself" might help. By focusing on her carefully crafted response to this important question, she was able to break her response down into phrases. It was easier to speak phrases slowly, allowing breaths between each phrase. She also forced herself to think of her response in advance then edit it until she forced her response to the desired length.

Diane was able to force herself to organize her thoughts so everything she wanted to say came out clearly, displaying her extraordinary experience rather than her powerful, sometimes overwhelming energy.

It is important to practice speaking slowly and calmly so your responses to interview questions demonstrate your internal confidence. Calmness makes you feel more confident and makes the listener confident in your abilities.

Think about our analogy to comedians. Two candidates can have the exact same experience. One speaks quickly, without an organized response. The other speaks calmly with a well-organized response, telling her story clearly and making the connection between her experience and the position available. Which one makes the better impression?

You root for the comedian who tells his story best, using the formula with a beginning, middle, and a punch line at the end. You root for the comedian who comes across with effortless grace, without displaying the hours of writing, editing, and practice, which go into his presentation.

Just like comedians, interviews are about impressions. Candidates who make a good impression are more likely to get what they want than a similarly qualified candidate who makes a poor impression.

Give yourself the edge with this proven formula for controlling the interview and making the best impression.

Chapter 11

Random Interview Questions

Listening Is Critical

Have you ever watched Wanda Sykes or Jimmy Fallon perform? They are masters. They know pretty much what they want to say. They prepare their act focused on the audience they expect to find that night. They have concepts, perhaps even fully formed paragraphs that they wrote, edited, and painstakingly rehearsed. Then they get on stage.

On stage, Wanda or Jimmy do not just recite what they prepared - like actors reciting Shakespeare. Comedians start out with the act they prepared but then they listen. Is it going over well? Which jokes are better received? What vibes are they getting from the audience? Where are the laughs? Then the performers adjust their act to reflect what the audience wants and needs.

Good comedians succeed because they listen to the audience and give the audience what they want - within the structure of what the comedian wants to talk about. Give and take. Give a little more of this and a little less of that based on what the audience wants. The comedian's goal is to make the audience laugh by giving the audience what it wants.

An interview is not that much different. Give and take. Give the interviewer more of this, less of that, based on what you hear and observe from the interviewer's reactions. Just like a comedian, listening is critical.

A well-structured response to "Tell me about yourself" is the start of your "act." It lays out an overview of your background so you can see what interests the interviewer (the audience). The interviewer (audience) responds with questions and physical responses from facial and vocal expressions that give you feedback on what he or she wants to talk about.

Then because you are so well prepared to give a little more of this and a little less of that, the interviewer (the audience) gets the experience he or she wants. They want to see a qualified candidate who will work well with the rest of the team. You want to give them what they want. By adjusting your comments (your act), you give the interviewer what they want to see about you. You become the ideal candidate.

Notice we are still telling the truth. Everything you say is always true. You can show a little more of this and a little less of that and still tell the truth. It will be the truth you want to share and the truth the interviewer wants to hear but still the truth.

One time I got a job offer even though no one asked me a single question beyond, "Tell about yourself." I answered this question at the beginning of five different interviews. After that, each interviewer proceeded to talk for at least an hour about what the interviewer wanted to talk about. I kept the conversation going in each interview by saying, "Really?", "Hmmmm," "yes," "Tell me more," and "I understand."

The interviewers at that company did not really know who I was or what I brought to the table. They liked me because I reflected what they wanted to hear back to them.

I learned a lot about the company. Here is what I learned:

- I learned all about the people I would be working with. I liked them a lot.
- I learned about the company's plans, goals, and aspirations. I thought I could fit in.
- I asked questions about financial results and got a little information.
- I learned about the people and union problems that I would have to work on if I took that job. I thought I could handle those issues.

Here is what the company learned about me:

- I am a good listener.
- They could get along with me.

Pretty much that was it. Because the interviewers talked so much, they did not know much about me. They did not know about my background, what motivates me, or whether I could do the job. But that did not matter to them. I was a good listener, they liked me, and that must have been enough for them. I got a job offer.

Listening was the key. By laying out my initial response then listening to figure out what was important to the interviewers I was able to reveal more of what they wanted to hear and less of what they did not want to hear. They did not want to hear about my background or the great accomplishments I could bring. They did not even want to hear about how I could solve their issues. By being quiet and letting them talk I did not undermine my chances with unimportant (to them) things like experience and qualifications.

In another situation, I met with Brian, the president of a very large company looking for a Director of Human Resources. After my response to "Tell me about yourself," he asked very specific questions about an accomplishment I mentioned. I selected this accomplishment because it directly related to what I understood to be his issue. Brian was very interested in the experiences and approaches I described, as I hoped he would be. Those stories provided the springboard to extensive discussions. We even planned the approach I would take if I were hired.

Listening was the key. I was able to discern from his questions the situations he was facing. I could tell stories about my experiences addressing those issues. He never came out and said, "I have this specific problem." I figured it out from the questions he asked and the items in my background he focused on. Then I gave him a little more of this and a little less of that so he saw the side of me I wanted him to see. I told the truth but it was the version of the truth he needed to know.

If I would have approached Brian the same way I approached some other company I would have been escorted out within minutes. If I told my stories without listening to Brian's questions, I might have lasted a little longer because my experience was applicable but I would have missed the nuances about working with Brian.

Listening and then adjusting my story to respond to my audience made the interview successful and got me the job. If I were unprepared, I would not have had the energy to listen to Brian. I knew what I wanted to say and I knew what I wanted Brian to know about me.

Because I was prepared, I could adjust on the spot in a way I would not have been able to do if I had to think up answers on the spot. I was not creating. I was adjusting. There is a very big difference between creating responses and adjusting responses.

Listening and adjusting responses to your audience make the difference between successful and unsuccessful interviews.

Preparation Lets You Observe and Anticipate

Imagine you are sitting across from an interviewer in a glass enclosed conference room. You selected a chair with your back to the windows so you can see outside the conference room into the main office area. You are prepared for this interview. You know what you want the interviewer to know about you. You are waiting to hear what he wants to know about you.

The interviewer kicks off with "Tell me about yourself" and then asks questions about your five words. "What do you mean by well organized?" You have a story prepared about each of your five words so you are feeling confident. Over the interviewer's shoulders, you see two people having a big argument over some paperwork. Hmmmm… That is very interesting. Store that tidbit away.

You tell your story about how well organized you are. Then the interviewer asks, "Tell me about a time you worked under a lot of pressure without a lot of resources." Ahhh... now it is making sense. This organization is having trouble. There is a lot of pressure and not a lot of resources. The situation is putting people on edge, causing friction among colleagues. That is very interesting.

You tell a story about how you worked once under a lot of pressure without excess resources. When it is your turn to ask questions, you know you want to talk about how the company allocates resources, how colleagues get along, what the team would say about the manager, and questions related to how goals are set. No need to say what you observed. Just ask the questions when it is your turn.

Because you prepared in advance for most of the questions you will be asked, the responses roll off your tongue and you are able to focus on what else is going on around you. You are confident and also able to observe what is going on around you so you can decide whether you want to work there or not.

"Tell me about yourself" provides basis for response to other questions.

You can use much of the information from your "Tell me about yourself" to respond to other questions. Consider some of Frequently Asked Questions that might come up.

What are your strengths?

When we asked you to consider five words that describe you, you are actually picking words that are your strengths. If those words were not important to the core of who you are you would have chosen different words.

Your response to the question, "What are your strengths?" should be one of your five words. Pick one that you think the interviewer would like to hear and tell a short story describing that strength in action.

Brenda selected the word "facilitator" as one of her five words. She knows that she loves to organize things and loves to get people to work with her to follow through on open items. She prepared a story about this word during her preparation for "Tell me about yourself." She did not use it yet. When asked about her strengths, she pulled up the story she prepared for the five words portion of "Tell me about yourself." It might sound like this:

> *I would say I am a facilitator. I am at my best when I make things happen to achieve a goal. For example, as a volunteer at the food pantry I figured out how to store and serve a large donation of eggs to make the best use of the donation. I described what we would do and got the team to make it happen.*

This answer is short and based on her preparation since the response to "Tell me about your strengths" is already built in "Tell me about yourself."

What is your weakness?

This question might substitute "developmental area" for "weakness." No need to think of a new response to this question. A weakness is just a strength gone to excess. Think about it. Pick one of your strengths and consider what happens when you put a lot of pressure on that strength.

Brenda knows that under a lot of pressure, her strength of facilitation, which is an extension of being well organized, can make her a little strident and quite forceful. She has been told this before. So the answer to this question can focus on facilitation gone overboard. She can use this opportunity to show how she has learned to cope with this "weakness." Her response might sound like this:

When I am under pressure, I get frustrated that people around me do not see the solution that I see. I tend to become more forceful. I have been told this can be annoying to people I work with. To control this tendency, when I am under pressure, I try very hard to explain what I am seeing and the advantages of the solution I propose. I slow down and ask people to repeat what they think I am saying to make sure we are on the same page. This approach works very well to get the team on the same page.

This answer does not include a story. But Brenda has a story to go with this. She says:

I led a team working on hurricane preparation and response after Hurricane Ivan. We had no time to spare because the building was damaged and our records were in jeopardy unless we responded immediately. I knew exactly what we should do but the team was scattered, distracted, and stressed. I gathered the group together and calmly explained the situation. I made sure everyone had coffee and a cookie to get them calmer. I took ideas from the team members. Then I explained the plan, incorporating the team's ideas right on the spot. Everyone nodded and repeated back the steps and individual responsibilities. Without that approach, I would have talked louder and more forcefully, overwhelming the team without accomplishing anything. With this approach, everyone did their part and we achieved the goal- we saved the records, and relocated business operations to a safe place according to the plan.

Brenda uses this story to acknowledge a strength gone to excess and the steps she takes to counter her excess (weakness). The story makes her look good by emphasizing an accomplishment related to the position she wants. Brenda uses "Tell me about yourself" to answer another FAQ and make herself look good at the same time. The interviewer will see her maturity, grasp of problems, and how well she works with her team, which is exactly what she wants the interviewer to see!

What do you want?

The answer to this question is part four of "Tell me about yourself." Clever, huh? When the interviewer asks this frequently asked question (FAQ), you go back to your preparation for part four and bring it up. You do not say, "As I said in my response to 'Tell me about yourself.'" You pretend that you just heard the question and just discovered the right answer off the top of your head.

A prepared Nathan 2.0 could pull this answer out of his Tell Me About Yourself Response:

> *I am looking for an accounting position that allows me to use my experience and my CPA credentials to stay organized. I know I can make a contribution.*

Nathan 2.0 should expect follow up questions digging deeper into the ideal position or his new CPA credentials. Simple and to the point. The interviewer will like the fact that Nathan 2.0 knows what he wants and is consistent throughout the interview.

John, the industrial engineer, would say,

I am looking for an industrial engineering position in logistics and supply chain supporting cost reductions and process simplification.

Sarah, the college professor, might say,

I am looking for a tenure track position in education at the graduate level utilizing online technology to teach active learning techniques.

The response must be specific and should match the opening you are interviewing for, just like your preparation for "Tell me about yourself."

What are your career objectives?

This is a variation on "What do you want?" Be prepared to expand a bit. You can talk about your longer-term objectives if it feels right. Your response can contain portions of your mission if that fits.

Katherine says,

I am looking for a position reporting to the president on a senior staff where I can solve problems with humor so the organization is successful."

This answer describes the kind of team she wants to work with, how she works, and the level at which she prefers to work. She does not have to give a title. She should never talk about her personal life.

Here are some bad answers to this question:

- I plan to retire in three years.
- I want to have a dozen kids and be supported by my husband in a big house in the suburbs.
- I want to travel around the world for two years then settle down in a job as the president of a big corporation.
- I plan to work for a few years to accumulate the funds then buy my own carpet cleaning franchise.

All of these responses might be true. That is fine. However, your answer to this question or questions like this should be related to the job you seek and should be business related, not personal. Never personal.

What motivates you?

This is a trick question. Interviewers are often looking for a specific answer. I have heard sales executives say they would never hire a sales person who did not answer this question by saying, "money." I think that is ridiculous, but my opinion is not important. Remember you want to give the version of the truth that the interviewer wants to hear.

If you are a sales person and motivated by something other than money, you might say "money" and the other thing that is your real motivator.

If you are not in sales, look to Part Three (Five Words) or Part Five (Why They Should Hire You) to pull a good answer.

Brenda would pull from her five words to respond like this:

I am motivated by the chance to organize chaos around me. This gives me a sense of accomplishment that I can use my skills to make the team better.

Brenda turns the interviewer's attention back to topics Brenda wants to discuss.

Describe your work style.

This is another trick question. The interviewer is looking less for an understanding of your work style and more to see if you will fit into the team. You should be honest because you want to be comfortable in the job and with the team but temper your honesty with what you have heard.

If you just heard a question about how you work under pressure and observed conflict among team members over the interviewer's shoulder, then you will want to respond with something about being easy to work with, if that is true.

Marissa's Story

Marissa is quiet and likes to work alone. She likes being responsible for her own work and not rely on a team. She has to be careful because most organizations want people who can work well with teams. She can work with teams but prefers to work alone.

Her response to this question might be:

I work well on a team but I really enjoy working alone and being responsible for my own results. When I worked on the Smith campaign, I worked with a team of six people. We divided the work and came together periodically to collaborate and consolidate our findings. This was a great work experience for me.

This response highlights her main interest in working alone but also illustrates how she can work with a group. It should be sufficient. Marissa does not want to work exclusively on a team so she will not be disappointed if she is not selected for exclusively team-oriented positions. Yet she does not want to exclude herself from positions with team interaction. Her response walks a fine line to keep her in the game until she decides whether the position is right for her.

What was your top accomplishment?

You prepared several accomplishments in your tool bag. You used one in Part Two of your Tell Me About Yourself Response. If this question comes up again, either you can elaborate on the accomplishment you previously mentioned or you can select another one that fits even better with the information you discerned and picked up by listening to the interviewer so far.

What would others say about you?

I love asking this question because candidates say the craziest things. I have heard candidates tell me about the big fight they had with a co-worker who refused to stop wearing cologne or the results of the candidate's last performance review.

A better answer is to go back to the five words in Part Three. You selected these words because they represent who you are. Your boss or co-workers probably noticed these things about you.

Katherine would pick out her problem solving skills and say,

My boss liked the way I listened and solved business problems based on the various bits of information I picked up from the rest of the team.

Temper your response to the position you are talking about and the vibes you are picking up from the interviewer.

Chapter 12

Behavioral Questions

We have said many times that most interviewers are not very well prepared because they are overworked and do not have much time. Some companies, often larger companies, do a great deal of training to help the hiring manager interview better.

One of the techniques involves a different kind of question, often called Behavioral Events Interviewing. It can have many abbreviations like STAR or SOARA. STAR stands for Situation, Task, Action, and Response. SOARA stands for Situation, Objective, Action, Results, and Aftermath (fromWikipedia.com).

The idea is that past behavior predicts future results. If you successfully handled a situation in the past, you should have learned from it and can apply what you learned to future situations. This interview training technique also requires the hiring managers ask the same questions of each candidate. They will often have a little stack of papers in front of them to guide them through the questions they are supposed to ask.

This technique has been around for a number of years in a futile effort to improve the way hiring managers conduct interviews. Most people interviewing candidates outside of Human Resources find this technique tedious. Sometimes if you share interesting information, you can see the hiring manager put their stack of papers aside and look at you. Then you know either the interview is over or the hiring manager sees you as a human worthy of further conversation.

There is nothing scary about these open-ended questions. You answer them with stories. Well-trained interviewers will often insist that you tell the entire story with all the parts before moving on to another question. It takes so long to answer these questions correctly that you might only get three or four of these questions in an hour interview. That is fine.

You can answer these questions with some of the background you include in your response to "Tell me a little about yourself," and the stories you already prepared. Answering this question requires a formula response. You want to tell stories that support the good qualities you want the interviewer to see that draw a line between your skills and experience and the job you want to get.

The story must have certain parts that form the beginning, middle, and end.

Sample Behavioral Question: Tell me about a time you worked under a lot of pressure with clients that complained all the time. (This is a real behavioral interview question from my past.)

> **Step 1: Situation** (The beginning) Describe the situation, task, or challenge you found yourself in that corresponds to the question asked. This must be very specific, not general. Who was involved? What trouble did this situation cause your company, team, customers depending on the story you want to tell? Business stories are best but sometimes the perfect story comes from your personal life.

Step 2: Action (The middle) What did you do about it? What was your role? What steps did you put in place to solve the problem? What alternatives did you consider? Even if you worked with a team, mention the team but talk about your role. What did YOU do to make this work? This is not bragging. It is telling a story that really happened and with which you were involved.

Step 3: Result (The end) What was the outcome or result? Did you meet your objectives? What did you achieve through those actions?

Step 4: What you learned. This is most important. It is ok if the story describes a failure as long as you learned something from it. The learning is critical. The learning should make you look good if possible.

This is not a complicated structure. It is not too much different from the format we suggest for telling stories. It should not be scary. You can prepare some of these responses in advance. The most important element is to provide a result and tie that result to something you want to show the interviewer.

Let us consider how this works for Jim.

Jim's Story

Jim is interviewing for a promotion from Financial Analyst to Financial Manager in another firm.

The interviewer asks: Tell me about a time when you were frustrated with your boss.

Jim picks a situation where his boss was putting a lot of pressure on him to get a report out but Jim was overwhelmed with work and frustrated that he could not get everything done. His response might sound something like this:

(**Situation**) I remember this time at XYC Company when I worked as a Financial Analyst. I worked with two other financial analysts under the Financial Manager, Susan. She was under a lot of pressure to complete a prospectus very quickly to predict how long it would take the new acquisition to begin showing profit. We were short-handed because so much was going on at the same time. It was very frustrating.

(**Action**) I got together with the other financial analysts and the acquisition project manager to see how we could juggle the tasks and assignments around so we could get everything done. Thomas, the project manager, liked this approach. The four of us came up with a different plan that I presented to Susan.

(**Result**) As a result, we were able to balance the workload among the financial analysts so we could meet all the deadlines and make Susan look good in front of the CFO.

(**Learned**) I learned that by working closely with my colleagues we could come up with a solution that put everyone at ease, especially my boss.

Jim chose a story that highlights his ability to work with colleagues to solve a problem. He looks like an enterprising person. It is not important to mention that Susan was a crazy lady and Jim is running as fast as possible away from her. That is not important to the story. The story makes Jim look good but does not do so at Susan's expense.

Notice the story does not take very long to tell. It has all the required components for a STAR or behavioral interview response. It also has all the components of the formula: a beginning, middle, and an end and what I learned.

Jim selects this story from one of his five words. Jim thinks of himself as proactive. He loves to solve problems. He used those two words in Part Three of his Tell Me About Yourself Response. He already prepared stories for each word. This was one of those stories! The Tell Me About Yourself Response works for you in yet another way!

The Secret to Behavioral Questions

Behavioral questions are usually connected to the "competencies" required in the job. Competencies are the knowledge, skill, and ability, or behavior expected on the job. Hopefully, the hiring manager identified the competencies he or she wants from the new hire before recruiting began. We can often find these competencies in the job description used during the hiring process.

Here are some competencies associated with a Wholesale Distribution Branch Manager from a real description of a real job. The ideal candidate has these competencies or characteristics or skills and abilities:

- Customer focus
- Decision making

- Delegating responsibilities
- Planning and organizing
- Aligning performance for success
- Sales ability / persuasiveness
- Stress tolerance

These abilities make sense for a management position like this. A Wholesale Distribution Branch Manager will lead a group of employees that interact with customers. We can anticipate that the hiring manager might ask questions about these abilities.

If you are interested in a position as a Wholesale Distribution Branch Manager, you have done your research and you think you have those abilities. You can make decisions, have a customer focus and understand how to delegate responsibilities. You can tell a story about your ability to do each one of these things. Some of these abilities might be among your five words! Therefore, you are already prepared.

Behavioral Questions sound different:

- The questions will be open ended. It is not possible to answer a behavioral question with "yes" or "no".

- Behavioral questions begin with a cue such as "Tell me about a time when…" or "Give me an example of …"

This is your cue to phrase your answer in the form of a story. Your response might begin, "I remember this time when…" or "Once at ABC Company we had a problem." Then you launch into your story that has a beginning, middle, end, and what you learned that relates specifically to the characteristic or competency hidden in the question.

Let us create some behavioral questions for the competencies required for a Wholesale Distribution Manager then figure out how to answer these questions for Tom, the manager we met in Chapter 2.

Questions about Planning and Organizing

- *What objectives were you expected to meet this year? What steps did you take to make sure you were making progress on all of them? NOTE: The question might also sound like this: Tell me about a time you had trouble meeting all your annual objectives and what did you do to make progress on all of them.*

Tom anticipates this question because he knows from experience that a Wholesale Distribution Branch Manager spends much of his day planning and organizing. He has many stories from his experience. He prepares one or two interesting stories that show him at his best. It might sound like this:

(Tom sets up the Situation) When I was at NCD Company, I was responsible for 5 warehouse employees 3 office employees and 3 sales people. In 2011, the company drastically changed the pricing philosophy to convert from cost based pricing to value based pricing. This big deal affected every aspect of the business. We received instructions from the home office but most of the work needed to be done at the local branch since we are responsible for our own P&L.

I got the team together to announce the changes and explain what this meant. (Tom begins to describe his Action). I set up regular education sessions with an expert from the home office. I worked closely with our top branch analyst and an analyst from the home office to understand the actual cost and market cost of our inventory. I was most interested in how our customers valued our products. We methodically changed our pricing approach.

Then we had to consider the impact on our customers. I worked with the sales team to create an implementation plan so customers would accept the new pricing. Then the sales people decided how they would approach the customers in the least disruptive manner.

As a team, we created a big project plan that showed each team members' responsibilities and estimated time to complete. We updated that plan regularly with the problems and accomplishments.

Using this process, we met the business goals for conversion and increased our gross margin by 15% that year. (Tom describes the Result).

This exciting project changed the face and results of our business. (Tom shares what he learned) I learned how important it is to involve the team in planning. The team did all the work but because I set a vision and expectations, they met the challenge very positively with a great result for our branch.

Tom's story begins with a situation and task, describes the action in the middle, and ends with the result or outcome. He concludes with what he learned so he can take the interviewer back to the main points he wants the interviewer to remember. His answer is not too long or detailed.

The interviewer is not interested in too many details. The story is just a vehicle for explaining how you handle the competency.

This is a very common behavioral question for any candidate who is interested in a position that requires a great deal of planning and organizing, including engineers, supply chain professionals and managers of all kind. If the position you are pursuing involves planning and organizing (and most positions do), think of a good answer to this question that includes the four steps.

Step 1 Situation

_____

_____

Step 2 Action

_____

_____

Step 3 Result

_____

_____

Step 4 Learned

_____

_____

Practice your answer aloud until the words flow out of your mouth smoothly. You might have to edit your response to make it feel right and to be certain you make the points you want to make.

Questions about Sales Ability or Persuasiveness

- _Describe a situation in which you had to use a different approach or perhaps several approaches because your initial approach failed to sell or persuade others._

You can anticipate this kind of question if you want to work in sales. People often learn more from failures than from successes so you can anticipate that someone might ask you about a failure. You should have a story prepared about your sales technique if you are in a sales field or a failure if you are in almost any other field.

Questions about Stress Tolerance

- *Every job produces different levels of stress. What was the most stressful aspect of your last job? How did you react to this stress?*

The interviewer will evaluate the stress described in your story to see if you can handle the incredible level of stress in the job at hand.

You might think it odd that a management job includes an ability to tolerate stress. Management jobs are very stressful. You have to deal with bosses, with requirements and objectives set by others, with employees, and often with customers. The situation is ripe for stress. If you are in management, you should expect questions about how you balance many objectives at once, how you handle stress, or how you handle difficult customers or employees. Come prepared with a toolkit of stories.

Here is another side benefit to coming prepared with a toolkit of stories. You can focus on why the interviewer is asking those particular questions.

Deliberate Questions

Interviewers choose to ask questions not only directly related to the available job but also questions that reflect the current work environment.

If they ask questions about stressful workplace, they probably have a stressful workplace. Otherwise, why would they waste your time and theirs with a question that is not important?

If they ask questions about difficult colleagues, a grumpy boss or colicky customers, they probably have a workplace with difficult colleagues, a grumpy boss or colicky customers.

If they ask questions about unethical demands from superiors, chances are they have had an unethical situation recently.

If they ask questions about working with few resources, lots of ambiguity, and overwhelming responsibilities, they probably work with few resources, lots of ambiguity, and overwhelming responsibilities. Otherwise, they would ask different questions.

When you are prepared, know what to say, and have lots of stories in your toolkit, you can listen to the question, select a story from your toolkit, and note the question in the back of your mind to review later. When it is your turn to ask questions, follow up to get more information about the workplace based on the questions you heard.

Chapter 13

Asking Your Own Questions

As you respond to the questions the interviewer asks, you will begin to develop a picture of the organization that is interviewing you. This is an excellent opportunity for you to ask specific questions about the company and its culture. That information is very helpful as you decide whether you want to work at this company. Remember, you are interviewing them as much as they are interviewing you.

Sydney's Story

Sydney was interviewing for a sales position. She heard these questions:

- *Tell me about a time your sales goals were set extremely high. How did you achieve these goals?*

- *Tell me about a time you worked with difficult customers. Describe one of the most stressful interactions you had with an internal or external customer. How did you react?*

Sydney pulled a few stories out of her toolkit and the interview continued but the behavioral questions she heard stuck with her. She wondered what kind of workplace this was, so when it was her turn to ask questions, Sydney asked these questions:

- How are sales goals set here?
- How much did sales goals increase last year for the average sales person?
- What was the increase for this territory?
- What results did this territory achieve compared to the annual sales goal last year?
- Are annual sales goals established based on the territory potential?
- Are sales goals are set arbitrarily?
- How much input does the sales person have on the sales goals?
- Are the sales goals set realistically?
- How viable is this territory?
- If the territory achieved 47% compared to sales goal but the goal increased by 200%

year over year, then you have a hint that
the sales goals are not set realistically
compared to the territory potential. This is
very important information.

- What sales results did the last person who
held this position achieve? Can I talk to him
or her?

Sydney wants to know whether the last person
was successful or not. If the last person still works
for the company, they might let you talk to that
person. That conversation will add more
information to aid your decision about whether
you want to work there. You want to learn why
the predecessor no longer works for the company,
especially if the person was terminated. This
information can be very valuable to you later
while deciding if this is the job or company for
you.

Sydney formulated her questions based on
observations she made during the interview. She
wanted to learn whether she could be successful in
this job. If not, she might not be interested. She
would not make any decisions during the
interview but she did give this information serious
consideration later.

During the interview, she was gathering information based on the questions she heard during the interview. The questions she heard were clues.

Being prepared with stories in response to 80% or more of the questions you might be asked allows you to focus your attention on observations:

- Why they are asking those particular questions?
- What kind of workplace is this?
- Will I enjoy working here?
- What do I think of these people?
- What is going on around me?

You will use your observations to gather information about what it is like to work in that company.

Chapter 14

Pull it All Together

At this point, you know:

- What you want
- How to confidently answer the main question "Tell me about yourself..." so you convey who you are and what you want
- How to describe your experience in stories
- How to answer behavioral questions

Let us consider how to own your next interview. To pull it all together we need to tie all the pieces together strategically.

Ben's Story

Ben is a recent college graduate who wants to be a real estate developer. He has all the education and internships he needs. He is absolutely unafraid of cold calling and as a result is able to get interviews.

He is uncomfortable during the interview because he feels unnatural.

He came to The Interview Doctor® for help.

We worked on his answer to "Tell me about yourself..." He identified his five words: eager, persistent, motivated, determined, and visual.

He developed stories around the five parts of this response including his five words, his accomplishments, and his goals.

Then we talked about the main characteristics or competencies that would make the person successful. The successful real estate developer is eager, persistent to get deals, determined to get what he wants, and have a plan with a vision of what he wants.

Ben saw that the characteristics for the job directly overlap his five words (his strengths). This gave him added confidence. We talked about ways to insert into his stories and responses the words that describe him so well and describe the characteristics of a successful real estate developer.

Ben went on an interview the next day. His response to "Tell me about yourself..." was a hit!

As we hoped, the interviewer asked follow up questions about the interesting tidbits Ben built into this Tell Me About Yourself Response. Ben sprinkled his conversation with the keywords describing a successful real estate developer. He shaped his stories with those words. The hiring manager ate it up! Ben got a job offer!

The secret to Ben's successful interview was preparation.

Preparation Makes You Confident

Confidence makes you calm. Calm, confident and courageous make you a great candidate! Here are some action steps to prepare for your interview:

1. Prepare your response to the foundational questions, "Tell me about yourself." Write down your responses. Practice aloud and edit until your response rolls off your tongue naturally.
2. Do the same with every question on the list of 30 most frequently asked questions. Use the information you developed in "Tell me about yourself" in your responses so you are consistent.

3. Create stories for each element of "Tell me about yourself" and the most frequently asked questions.

4. Consider all the knowledge, skills, abilities, and behavior expected of the position you want. Think of stories to demonstrate that you have those knowledge, skills, abilities, and behavior. Write down those stories.

5. Get feedback. Find a friend or family member willing to listen to you and give you feedback. Videotape yourself and watch your mannerisms. Make changes and adjustments based on your observations. Your goal is to look as confident as you feel inside.

6. Keep your typed, written responses in your portfolio so you can review your responses and stories prior to every interview. This puts your preparation in the front of your mind before you walk into the building, making you calm and confident.

7. Practice aloud until it rolls off your tongue naturally. A good rule of thumb is to practice until the person listening to you stops laughing.

8. Have a great handshake and make good eye contact to make a good impression

from the beginning. Be nice to everyone you meet including the janitor and receptionist. Smile.

9. Listen and observe the hiring manager to understand where to place emphasis. Adjust your stories and manner to mirror or reflect what interests the hiring manager.

10. Listen to the questions you are asked. Ask follow up questions to gather information about what it is like to work with those people at that company.

You can use these techniques whenever you meet new people - while networking, at meetings, at parties and whenever someone asks you about yourself.

Be prepared, know what you want to say, and why you want to say it; preparation is the key to a successful interview!

Discussion Questions

Everyone has to interview at one time or another in their life. Even a discussion with a banker about a mortgage is an interview of a sort. Interviewing is an important life skill that you must learn. Preparing alone is problematic since an interview always involves two people. We can learn a great deal from other people's experiences that we can apply to our own experiences.

We encourage you to discuss this book and your interview preparation with others who are having a similar experience. Working together increases camaraderie and leverages the strengths of the individual across the group. If you are not already part of a job seekers group, find one in your community and attend regularly. Toastmasters is also a great forum for practicing your interview responses.

Here are some questions to consider about interviewing. You might find these questions interesting to discuss with your job seekers group.

1. Did you find it difficult to work on the exercises? Which exercises were the most difficult and why? What are some of the obstacles you found in doing the exercises?
2. Think about the Five Words exercise. Why is the fifth word so difficult to identify? Did you

have any trouble thinking of five words? Share some stories about how the five words represent your strengths.

3. What is the impact of working on interviewing skills alone? What are some reasons we resist preparing for interviews? Do you find this same struggle in preparing for other life experiences?

4. Tell me about a time you heard a behavioral questions. What did you do? Were you prepared? How did you respond? After thinking about that question for a while, how would you answer it in a way that puts you in a better light?

5. Think about your past interviews. What questions do you believe you answered badly? What made that question so challenging? After working through this book, how would your response change?

6. Describe your worst interview. What went wrong? What would you change?

7. Which of the characters described in this book do you identify with the most? What is it about that story that resonates with you factually or emotionally?

8. Regarding Jaxson's story, do you understand the hiring manager's perspective? How can Jaxson's experience help you on your next interview?

9. Go to YouTube and look up a Jimmy Fallon monologue. How does he change his delivery based on the audience's reaction? You might have to watch it a few times to see him listening. Identify the moment when you know he is changing his plan in order to play to the audience's laughter.

10. How would you respond to an interview question about your career goal if the position you were interviewing for was not the ultimate career or role you want?

11. What do you think about Nathan 2.0? How did his responses the second time differ from the first interview? If you are a manager, have you ever interviewed someone who made a terrible impression? What did you do?

About The Interview Doctor, Inc. ®

Do the stories in this book sound familiar? Have you been in the same position as these people looking for a job? Are you at your wits end?

The Interview Doctor® can show you a better way.

The Interview Doctor® can save you time and effort, moving your job search ahead by miles so you can land the job you love. We have the insight because we have the personal experience finding jobs and the business experience of hiring people. We know how you feel. We know what employers are looking for. We know how to break through those barriers with the right techniques to get the job you love.

We coach candidates via phone or in person - our services are available when and where you need them.

Shorten your job search. Find the job you love. Get the answers you need with personal job search coaching from The Interview Doctor®.

Become the one of the success stories. Working with The Interview Doctor® you will see results!

- Know your story and how to use it to get a job offer

- Know the important pieces to include in your resume

- Break through the Phone Screen barrier and land the job interview

- Understand how to act and what to say in the actual interview

All of these pieces play an important part in landing the job offer. When you go through our Job Interview Coaching process you will learn how to adjust your job search tactics and improve your results – resulting in job offers and landing the job you love.

Contact The Interview Doctor® and get the help you need with your Job Interview and Search.

Katherine Burik is an energetic and creative leader with a service focus to human resources. She has specific expertise in strategic human resource planning and coaching leadership teams to improve performance and results.

The Interview Doctor® sprang from Katherine's observation, based on her human resource experience and work with recruiters that candidates need to improve their interviewing skills. She coaches candidates looking for jobs, and speaks frequently to groups about career development and successful job search techniques. Her thoughts about job search appear regularly in The Interview Doctor® blog.

In her previous life as Vice President or Director of Human Resources at several businesses in Chicago and Northeast Ohio, Katherine reported to the President and CEO, responsible for the entire array of human resource functions. She has been laid off more times than most people she knows. Contrary to public opinion, being laid off can be liberating!

Katherine is a member of Toastmasters International; the Society of Human Resource Managers; the American Society of Training and Development; and the Worldwide Association of Business Coaches.

She earned her BA in History from Northwestern University and MS in Industrial Relations from Loyola University of Chicago. She has been certified as a Senior HR Professional by the Society of Human Resource Managers and is certified as a Registered Corporate Coach.

Dan Toussant is a human resource professional with over 20 years of leadership experience, specializing in management and professional recruiting. He speaks regularly to groups about the job-seeking process, and coaches professionals of any age one-on-one regarding interviewing skills, resume preparation, and career transition. He serves as the co-editor of The Interview Doctor Blog, and teams with his business partner, Katherine Burik, and other HR professionals in this job-interviewing skills, career-coaching collaborative, The Interview Doctor®.

Dan holds a Master's Degree in Education from Kent State University and a Bachelor's Degree in English from Boston College.

He is the beneficiary of some rather unique job promotions and changes in his professional life. Staying in his hometown and still working to advance his career has led to some interesting opportunities including nine years as HR Consulting Leader with a regional CPA firm, and now as a Professional Recruiter and Job-

Interviewing-Skills Webinar/Seminar Presenter and Coach.

He is an active member of Toastmasters International; Business Networking International (BNI); and the Society of Human Resource Management.

Connect with us: We want to connect with you on LinkedIn individually and at our LinkedIn Group, Job Search Check-Up. See how our contacts can help you in your job search!

Call the Interview Doctor® today at 800-914-7349! Sign up to receive our newsletter and blog at http://jobinterviewcoaching.org/contact/.

References

A Man Walks Into A Bar (n.d.). Ultimate collection of jokes and one-liners. Retrieved from http://www.manwalksintoajoke.com

About.com (n.d). Advice for comedians breaking into stand up. Retrieved from http://comedians.about.com/od/breakingin/tp/breakintostandup10tips.htm

Wikipedia (n.d). SOARA. Retrieved from http://en.wikipedia.org/wiki/SOARA

Wikipedia (n.d.). Situation-Task-Action-Results. Retrieved from http://en.wikipedia.org/wiki/Situation,_Task,_Action,_Result

Preview of

The Job Seeker Manifesto

The Job Search Marketing Plan

Declare to the World How

You Will Find Your Next Job!

Chapter 2

Job Search Marketing Plan

Every project has a plan. Every day has a plan, even if the plan is to have no plan.

Most Saturday mornings you wake up and probably think for a moment about what you want to do on the weekend. Maybe you need to go to the grocery store, get more dog food, wash the car, and visit your mom. Many people scribble notes on a scrap of paper with the stuff to pick up at the grocery store, maybe the order you want to do the chores. And voila, you have a plan!

The kind of plan you outline for yourself is a reflection of your personal style. It could be as simple as a scrap of paper or as complex as a multi-page project plan with a Gantt chart. But everyone has a plan.

Non-plans do not help

Every job seeker has a plan. It is just that some "plans" are vague, unformed, and unproductive. Let us call that a "non-plan." It is a plan, yes, but mostly ineffective; a non-plan is exactly the kind of plan that guarantees your job search takes forever.

In a non-plan job search, the candidate, let's call him Henry, checks the newspaper (maybe the real paper kind) and perhaps the ad consolidators on the Internet for jobs related to his/her job function. Henry sends out resumes in response to the ads. Then sits back and waits for the phone to ring. He gets more and more frustrated. Henry watches his unemployment checks wither away along with his savings. His embarrassment over his predicament makes him second-guess his every move. His confidence takes a nose-dive. If he is called for an interview, Henry barely keeps his chin off his shoes apologizing for his very existence, not listening, and not knowing how to display his skills and background in a way that makes him stand out against his competition. Henry and others like him can be out of work for a long, long time.

Plans are just lists of choices and decisions that must be made. The candidate with a "non-plan" made specific choices along the way. Unfortunately, they are choices and decisions that sidetracked the search. Let's consider:

- Choosing to answer ads instead of more effective search techniques
- Not really knowing what he wants or where to find it
- Not effectively using his time
- Not understanding what he offers employers or how to express it
- Allowing his situation to impact his self-confidence

A "non-plan" is a bad plan. Do yourself a favor and make a real plan that works for you instead of against you.

Plans have steps

According to *A Guide to the Project Management Body of Knowledge* (PMBOK Guide) from the Project Management Institute, a project plan is a process by which someone accomplishes a goal. You must understand the goal and decide which steps are necessary to achieve the goal.

Your plan may be simple or complex with many details. At a minimum, to get where you want to go you must know what you want and what you are willing to do to get it. It is also good to understand why that goal is the right goal for you.

A plan is like a map. If you do not have a map, you are traveling blind.[1] You might get there eventually but there will be a lot of costly twists and turns in the road, costing money, time, or energy. With

---

[1] [1]Berry, T. (2008). Who needs a business plan. Bplans Blog. Retrieved from http://articles.bplans.com/writing-a-business-plan/who-needs-a-business-plan/47

a map, you know where you are going, which roads get you there faster, and you can recognize the right place when you are there.

Businesses put together marketing plans to sell cereal, services, or machinery. They want to understand who is the competition, who is likely to buy this product, how much can it be sold for, where can it be sold, who are the people to talk to about buying the product, and other important information about the marketplace and the buyers. Then they measure themselves against the key milestones to see how well they accomplish the goal.

A **Job Search Marketing Plan** for a job seeker is a marketing plan in which the product to be sold is you. It is amazing how job seekers, even those in sales and marketing, overlook this simple idea. You are the product.[2]

Scott's Story

Scott was an Interview Doctor® client who specialized in sales. His job search was stalled and he did not understand why. He applied for job after job in his targeted field but nothing happened. He was starting to think it was his age or the way he dressed, a sign that his extended search was wearing on his confidence.

After talking with him for a short while about his goals and interests and about marketing in general he stopped talking for a second. He said, "Are you telling me that a job search is just like

[2] Fleishner, M. (1999). Ten key components of a marketing plan. Business Know How. Retrieved from http://www.businessknowhow.com/marketing/marketing-plan.htm.

*sales? Have I missed the point this whole time? If
so then I already know how to do this."*

*It occurred to him that the techniques that he
used every day to market and sell truck parts were
exactly the same techniques he could use to sell
himself to a new employer. He got off the phone
with renewed excitement and confidence. A week
later he called with the good news; he found a job!
In that short time after our call he identified his
potential marketplace and contacts, started calling
his contacts, renewed a relationship with a former
customer and was offered a job!*

It doesn't always happen as neatly as it did with
Scott but the point is the same. With a plan, you can
understand your marketplace.

Stephen Covey, in his groundbreaking book *The 7
Habits of Highly Effective People*[3], says that highly
effective people begin with the end in mind (Habit #2).
Begin with a clear picture of where you are now and
where you are going. In this way, your steps always
take you in the correct direction – the direction that
takes you to your goal.

You must understand what you want in order to
put all your energy to finding *it* then convincing the
people who own it that they should give it to you. So,
your plan begins with a goal and has steps along the
way to achieving the goal.

Individual plans may vary but essentially the
steps include:

[3] Covey, S.R. (2004). The 7 habits of highly effective people: Powerful lessons in personal change. New York: Free Press.

1. **Goal** – what do you want, what does it look like, where is it located (in general), why is this important to you, what will it feel like when you get it

2. **Research** – which companies and people can you talk to about that job

3. **Understand** what you have to offer – why are you the right person for this kind of a job

4. **Prospect** – talk to as many people and companies as you can until you find people willing to talk with you about your goal

5. **Make your case** – clearly explain the fit, build relationships until they find you irresistible

6. **Close the deal** - without a plan, you will wander all over. We frequently hear from candidates who have no plan.

Lila's Story

Lila is a boating friend I see in the summer. In May, on the first weekend at the boat, I asked how she was doing. She explained she had been laid off from her job at a doctor's office. She submitted application after application over the winter but got no response. Her plan, if you can call it a plan, was to respond to ads until something good happened. I asked what she wanted. She was willing to take almost anything.

How long do you think it will take Lila to get a job? Using her current approach, it will take Lila a very long time. She did no planning, she does not know what she wants, she does not know who to talk to or where to find the right job, and she is not using methods that will produce the result she wants. It takes a long time to get somewhere if you don't know where you going or how to get there.

Preview of

The Job Seeker Manifesto

RESUMES 3.0:

Tools to Find Your Next Job!

You can often tell how old someone is by his or her perspective of resumes. In the "olden days," say 15 or 20 years ago, resumes - summaries describing an individual's last few jobs and education - were typed or printed on special fancy paper purchased from the local stationery store. Laid off employees might attend an outplacement workshop to develop a final resume. At the end of the day, they received 50 copies of their new resume, printed on nice paper to begin their job search. Then off went the prospective candidate to hand out resumes and find a job.

Young people reading this are muttering to themselves, "Typed?" "Fancy paper?" "Stationery store?" What the heck does that mean?

It is a sign of the times that things have changed so much so quickly. Business has changed. The world has changed. Resumes have changed too.

You no longer need to find a secretary to type your resume professionally. You do not need special paper from a special stationary store (translation: stationary = paper) to use exclusively for business purposes.

I still have printed copies of old resumes in my file cabinet. Maybe you do too. If you do, then you probably are one of the parents who advise their children to seek out a professional to write their resume. Those parents believe that a fancy, printed resume these days is the ticket to a new job; they still believe that resumes are static and must be professionally prepared.

Do not get me wrong. Part of our service is writing resumes for people. We are glad to do it. However, technology has changed the world. As a result, resumes have a different role in today's job search.

This book explores the new role of resumes in the 3.0 generation. Resumes are one of many tools required by job searchers. However, they are not necessarily the centerpiece of today's job search as they were in the past. Your job search is flexible; it is personalized to your interests. Therefore, to support that job search, your tools must be flexible as well. We will look at resumes as a part of the strategic toolbox you will assemble for your job search.

What Is a Resume?

"Resume" is a French noun meaning "to continue." The job search resume is a description of your employment past and your goals for your employment future.

Since a job search is a continuation of employment from one employer or job to another it makes sense that, in your continuing career progression, you need tools to describe what you bring to the table from your past that will make you successful in the future.

The resume provides the rationale for a transition between old and new employment. Your experiences define you and support your future goals.

Resumes Then

In the old days, a resume was critical as the main way to tell people about you. Resumes used to be static, typed documents created and utilized in a manner that reflected the times. Professional secretaries typed resumes on a typewriter because that is what was available. Resumes were professionally printed on heavy bond paper that might have a nice watermark on it. We purchased extra sheets of the same paper to use for cover letters and matching mailing envelopes. We picked up the completed resumes at the stationary store or print shop in a clean brown bag where the resume stayed until you lovingly pulled one out to mail with a typed cover letter to people who might be interested in learning more about you.

If you were interested in two different areas, then you wrote up two different resumes. Changing these static resumes required retyping and reprinting. That meant getting it right the first time was very important. This kind of resume was the main method of presenting yourself and your experience to others in a position to hire you.

Not any longer. The world is different today.

Today almost everyone has a computer, knows how to type, and can print directly on a good printer in their home office. That means the ability to produce a resume on the spot has changed. The ability to type and print yourself means you can produce a resume custom designed to respond to the specific position available. Each resume can highlight specific experiences that correspond to the specific position. No more static printed resumes safely stored in a brown bags waiting for the proper moment.

In the days before social media, your resume was the only way to describe yourself to potential employers. If you wanted an employer to know about your background you gave them a written resume. There was nothing else. Today a paper resume may not even be necessary. You can easily get a job without a paper resume. There are so many more ways to tell your story.

"Resume" Today

A resume remains a tool, part of your strategic personal marketing plan. However, the old paper resume is only one of many tools at your disposal to share your background and experiences with potential employers.

We use the word "resume" loosely these days. A resume is not just a written document.

A resume can be paper or virtual now. A virtual resume allows you to expand beyond the margins of two sheets of fancy bond paper to tell the reader what you want and why you should have it. It is another way to tell your story. This new kind of "resume" is a consistent reflection of the person you want people to see whether they encounter you in social media outlets like LinkedIn or Facebook or meet you in person at a networking event or in a formal interview with a paper resume in your hand.

We usually start creating your "resume" with the actual paper resume. Today almost everyone has a computer, knows how to type, and can print directly on a good printer in their home office. That means the ability to produce a resume on the spot has changed. The ability to type and print yourself means you can produce a resume custom designed to respond to the specific position available. Each resume can highlight specific experiences that correspond to the specific position. No more static printed resumes safely stored in a brown bags waiting for the proper moment. The ability to change the focus of your experience, and the discipline of editing your experiences down to a one or two page format helps identify the most important information to support your goals. LinkedIn and social media options flesh out more details that might not be included in the paper document.

www.ingramcontent.com/pod-product-compliance
Lightning Source LLC
Chambersburg PA
CBHW050124210326
41519CB00015BA/4096